T0329146

Cambridge Elements ≡

Elements in the Philosophy of Religion
edited by
Yujin Nagasawa
University of Birmingham

ONTOLOGICAL ARGUMENTS

Tyron Goldschmidt

CAMBRIDGE
UNIVERSITY PRESS

CAMBRIDGE
UNIVERSITY PRESS

University Printing House, Cambridge CB2 8BS, United Kingdom

One Liberty Plaza, 20th Floor, New York, NY 10006, USA

477 Williamstown Road, Port Melbourne, VIC 3207, Australia

314–321, 3rd Floor, Plot 3, Splendor Forum, Jasola District Centre, New Delhi – 110025, India

79 Anson Road, #06–04/06, Singapore 079906

Cambridge University Press is part of the University of Cambridge.

It furthers the University's mission by disseminating knowledge in the pursuit of education, learning, and research at the highest international levels of excellence.

www.cambridge.org
Information on this title: www.cambridge.org/9781108711845
DOI: 10.1017/9781108686990

© Tyron Goldschmidt 2020

First published 2020

A catalogue record for this publication is available from the British Library.

ISBN 978-1-108-71184-5 Paperback
ISSN 2399-5165 (online)
ISSN 2515-9763 (print)

Cambridge University Press has no responsibility for the persistence or accuracy of URLs for external or third-party internet websites referred to in this publication and does not guarantee that any content on such websites is, or will remain, accurate or appropriate.

Ontological Arguments

Elements in the Philosophy of Religion

DOI: 10.1017/9781108686990
First published online: October 2020

Tyron Goldschmidt

Author for correspondence: Tyron Goldschmidt, tyron.golds@gmail.com

Abstract: Proving the existence of God is a perennial philosophical ambition. An armchair proof would be the jackpot. Ontological arguments promise as much. This Element studies the most famous ontological arguments from Anselm, Descartes, Plantinga, and others. While the verdict is that ontological arguments do not work, they get us entangled in fun philosophical puzzles, from philosophy of religion to philosophy of language, from metaphysics to ethics, and beyond.

Keywords: ontological arguments; God; philosophy of religion; metaphysics

ISBNs: 9781108711845 (PB), 9781108686990 (OC)
ISSNs: 2399-5165 (online), 2515-9763 (print)

Contents

1 Introduction

1.1 Armchairs

Ontological arguments are arguments for the existence of God. What makes them distinct is that they are supposed to be *armchair* proofs. The premises are all supposed to be

- knowable *a priori*: knowable independently of any particular empirical observations, or
- analytically true: true in virtue of definitions and concepts, or
- necessarily true: true no matter how the world might have differed.

Or *something* like that. The terms are hard and counterexamples loom.

Contrast cosmological and design arguments for the existence of God. For example:

- Some cosmological arguments try to show that God exists on the premise that the universe began to exist, and so must have a supernatural cause (see Craig 2018).
- Some design arguments try to show that God exists on the premise that the laws of nature are finely tuned to allow for life (see Collins 2018).

These are not armchair proofs. Their premises appeal to detailed empirical evidence about the beginning of the universe or the fine-tuning of natural laws. They are much more hostage to scientific discovery than ontological arguments are. But, from the slightest premises, ontological arguments try to get us to the most sublime conclusion.

Graham Oppy prefers to define ontological arguments in terms of their historical descent from the original ontological argument of Anselm of Canterbury (1033–1109): "what is distinctive of ontological arguments is that their formulation has the right kind of connection to Anselm's argument" (2018: 11). True enough, though we might imagine something worth calling an *ontological argument* that is historically divorced from Anselm – one of the arguments covered in this Element (in Section 5) might count as such.

Maybe the best we can do is to classify ontological arguments by a kind of family resemblance between them. At least, I cannot give a more precise definition or general description of ontological arguments. But that will not matter to the presentation and evaluation of what have traditionally been classified as ontological arguments.

1.2 God

Ontological arguments try to prove that there is a greatest conceivable being or a greatest possible being or a perfect being – or *something* like that. And then such a being is supposed to turn out to be

- omnipotent: all-powerful,
- omniscient: all-knowing, and
- omnibenevolent: all-good.

Or *something* like that. For the most part, this is what we mean by *God* in what follows. The scriptures and traditions of different religions often point towards such a being, even if they do not explicitly mention omnipotence, omniscience, or omnibenevolence; the Jewish, Christian, and Muslim traditions are full of awesome praise of the power, knowledge, and goodness of God. The conclusion of ontological arguments is then usually religiously robust: it gives us a quite detailed picture of God that fits with religious traditions (though a more modest ontological argument is treated in Section 5).

Contrast, again, cosmological and design arguments. They are usually supposed to show one or other divine attribute – that there is a first cause or an intelligent designer – but not the perfect package of omnipotence, omniscience, and omnibenevolence. However, some arguments for particular religions might point to even more detailed conclusions than do ontological arguments (see Goldschmidt 2019, since no one else is going to be citing me).

Proving the existence of God is a perennial philosophical ambition. An armchair proof would be the jackpot. And there are other philosophical benefits besides. Yujin Nagasawa (2017: 33–35) advertises ontological arguments as answers to the big question of why there is anything at all: Why is there something rather than nothing? Most ontological arguments would prove the existence of a being that could not have failed to exist. There is, then, something rather than nothing because there *had* to be something – nothingness turns out to be impossible (compare Lowe 1998: chapter 12; Coggins 2010).

1.3 History

Ontological arguments have a distinguished pedigree and are about as famous as any philosophical arguments. Anselm formulated the first and most famous ontological argument around 1077. As armchair proofs, the arguments have since attracted thinkers of a mathematical bent, such as

- René Descartes (1596–1650), discoverer of Cartesian geometry,
- Gottfried Leibniz (1646–1716), discoverer of the calculus, and
- Kurt Gödel (1906–78), of incompleteness theorem fame.

The arguments also have distinguished detractors. Anselm's argument was immediately met with the criticisms of the monk Gaunilo, who liked every part of Anselm's book except the proof. Other major critics of ontological arguments include

- Thomas Aquinas (1225–74), the most famous medieval theologian,
- David Hume (1711–76), the most famous early modern skeptic, and
- Immanuel Kant (1724–1807), a very hard read.

These critics promise very general objections against any such argument. But others settle for less ambitious objections.

Contemporary proponents of ontological arguments include Jonathan Lowe, Yujin Nagasawa, and Alvin Plantinga, and contemporary critics include Graham Oppy, William Rowe, and Peter van Inwagen. This list is *very* incomplete, as are the others. We will meet some of the main historical and contemporary proponents and opponents of ontological arguments as we go along.

The proponents of the arguments listed here are mostly Christian, Western, and male. Anselm was not translated into Hebrew or Arabic for the medieval Jewish and Muslim philosophical traditions, and ontological arguments have since attracted much less attention from Jewish, Muslim, and other philosophers than from Christian philosophers. The arguments from the Muslim philosophers, Avicenna (980–1037) and Mullah Sadra (1571–1636), are sometimes taken to be ontological. But I am inclined to count Avicenna's argument (see McGinnis 2011) as a cosmological argument, and I do not understand Sadra's argument (see Rizvi 2019).

1.4 Outline

There is as much literature on ontological arguments as on any argument in philosophy. For the purposes of a short book, some simplicity must be imposed. I present and evaluate some influential ontological arguments and some influential objections – along with some not so influential but interesting arguments and objections. The focus and order are the arguments of

- Anselm in Section 2,
- Descartes in Section 3,
- Plantinga in Section 4,

- Lowe in Section 5, and
- a quick digest of other ontological arguments in Section 6.

And I have followed a neat pattern throughout of

- presenting the arguments with numbered premises,
- explaining the arguments, and then
- leveling objections to the arguments, along with replies to the objections.

But the order is somewhat contrived: points made about one argument often bear on others, as I will point out.

I also present the main arguments in the same kind of standard form throughout. Even where I quote an argument another author has put in a standard form, I often renumber the premises and reformat slightly for the sake of clarity and consistency. I note the editing in the citation.

1.5 Verdict

My verdict: ontological arguments should not persuade. The persuasiveness of any argument depends on

- how many people it should persuade, and
- the degree to which it should persuade them (see Rasmussen 2018: 193).

Some arguments should give anyone considering them carefully enough absolute certainty of the conclusion. Proofs of the Pythagorean theorem are examples. Some arguments should not move anyone even an iota. Ontological arguments fall somewhere between these extremes, but in my view, they are much closer to the unfortunate end. At least, this is unfortunate for me: I would love a beautiful armchair proof for a conclusion that I – as an Orthodox Jew – accept. I will explain which criticisms of ontological arguments work in the sections that follow.

There is nothing special about ontological arguments here: virtually no substantive argument in philosophy works (see van Inwagen 2006: lecture 3; Lycan 2019). Nevertheless, ontological arguments are wonderful: they get us entangled in so many other philosophical puzzles, from philosophy of religion to philosophy of language, from metaphysics to ethics, and beyond – more so, I think, than any other argument does. As Plantinga puts it:

> [M]any of the most knotty and difficult problems in philosophy meet in this argument. Is existence a property? Are existential propositions – propositions of the form *x exists* – ever necessarily true? Are existential propositions about what they seem to be about? Are there, in any respectable sense of "are,"

some objects that do not exist? If so, do they have any properties? Can they be compared with things that do exist? These issues and a hundred others arise in connection with Anselm's argument. (1974: 85)

While my verdict is pessimistic, I hope this book shows the fruitfulness of thinking about ontological arguments.

Bertrand Russell tells us that "[t]he argument does not, to a modern mind, seem very convincing, but it is easier to feel convinced that it must be fallacious than it is to find out precisely where the fallacy lies" (2004: 536). Russell wrote in a philosophical climate much more inimical to philosophical theology than contemporary philosophy is. But I would bet the sentiment remains. Plantinga, who is not at all inimical to this business, similarly tells us:

> At first sight Anselm's argument is remarkably unconvincing if not downright irritating; it looks too much like a parlor puzzle or word magic. [And yet] it is profoundly difficult to say what, exactly, is wrong with it. Indeed, I do not believe that any philosopher has ever given a cogent and conclusive refutation of the ontological argument In Its various forms. (1974: 85–86)

While my verdict is pessimistic, none of my preferred objections rule out the possibility of a victorious ontological argument. In my view, the objections of Hume and Kant – objections that try to forever rule out the possibility – are not so powerful. So maybe a victorious ontological argument will emerge. Besides, maybe there are rebuttals to my preferred objections; who do I think I am anyhow? But there is also the risk that some new objection, as devastating as general, will emerge.

1.6 Audience

This book assumes no prior understanding of ontological arguments. The literature is canvassed, and the main ideas are distilled. The arguments and objections are simplified, at least as far as I can simplify them without sacrificing important details. But I introduce some cutting-edge ideas and some original ideas. I just don't throw readers into the deep end. I aim for a wide audience, from interested laymen to philosophy professors. I suspect that a lot of my audience will be philosophy students, undergraduate and graduate ("a lot" being very relative when writing on philosophy). To aid understanding, I make

- a lot of
- use of
- bullet points,

as you have already noticed. Except in this case, these offset crucial definitions, principles, and so on, and help readers identify them and return to them if need be. They also look pretty to me.

1.7 Further Reading

Readers can follow my book without reading anything else on ontological arguments, including the primary sources; I quote from them liberally. But I hope that the book will spark interest in further study. For readers interested in delving more into ontological arguments, the following are especially recommended:

- Oppy (2018) – various authors study diverse ontological arguments;
- Szatkowski (2012) – various authors study diverse ontological arguments;
- Oppy (1995) – surveys and rejects diverse ontological arguments; and
- Nagasawa (2017) – defends ontological arguments from Anselm and Plantinga.

2 Anselm

2.1 Proslogion

Different ontological arguments have been discovered in or read into Anselm (see, e.g., Malcolm 1960). The main one is in his *Proslogion*, chapter 2:

> Now we believe that you are something than which nothing greater can be thought. So can it be that no such being exists, since "The fool has said in his heart, 'There is no God'"? (Psalm 14:1, 43:1) But when this same fool hears me say "something than which nothing greater can be thought," he surely understands what he hears; and what he understands exists in his understanding, even if he does not understand that it exists [in reality]. . . . So even the fool must admit that something than which nothing greater can be thought exists at least in the understanding, since he understands this when he hears it, and whatever is understood exists in the understanding. And surely that than which a greater cannot be thought cannot exist only in the understanding. For if it exists only in the understanding, it can be thought to exist in reality as well, which is greater. So if that than which a greater cannot be thought exists only in the understanding, then the very thing than which a greater *cannot* be thought is something than which a greater *can* be thought. But that is clearly impossible. Therefore, there is no doubt that something than which a greater cannot be thought exists both in the understanding and in reality. (Anselm 1995: 7; also see Logan 2016)

Anselm proceeds to argue that something than which nothing greater can be thought cannot be less than omnipotent, omniscient, and omnibenevolent. The rest of the *Proslogion* works out a detailed understanding of these attributes (for trouble with such a program, see Speaks 2018; for a general study of Anselm, see Visser & Williams 2008).

2.2 Interpretation

The passage is pretty but tricky. Richard Dawkins notes that "[a]n odd aspect of Anselm's argument is that it was originally addressed not to humans but to God himself, in the form of a prayer (you'd think that any entity capable of listening to a prayer would need no convincing of his own existence)" (2006: 104; see Williams 2016 on Anselm's attempt to combine two styles of writing). On the same basis, Karl Barth (1960) goes so far as to say that Anselm is not trying to prove the existence of God at all.

But Anselm is explicit that he was searching for and found "a single argument that needed nothing but itself alone for proof, that would by itself be enough to show that God really exists" (1995: 2). Anselm has faith. But – as per the original title of the *Proslogion, Fides Quaerens Intellectum* – his faith is in search of understanding. As Ermanno Bencivenga puts it for Anselm:

> I *know* that God exists. ... I know it from the best possible source – from revelation. ... But still, I am a human being, and reason plays an important role for me. It gives me pleasure to see how the various tenets of my faith harmonize with one another, how what I know to be the case could not possibly be otherwise, how it is not just true but also *reasonable*. (1993: 6)

Anselm has an argument. And the argument has many interpretations. I think that the following captures what is going on in Anselm, in a close enough order and making all the premises explicit. Instead of repeating the long phrase "that than which a greater cannot be conceived" over and over again, we can abbreviate it by the term *GOD*. Thus:

1. "GOD" is understood. (Premise)
2. If "GOD" is understood, GOD exists in the understanding. (Premise)
3. Even if GOD exists only in the understanding, it can be conceived to exist in reality. (Premise)
4. GOD is greater if it exists in reality than if it exists only in the understanding. (Premise)
5. It is impossible to conceive of something greater than GOD. (Premise)
6. If GOD exists in the understanding, then GOD exists only in the understanding or in the understanding and in reality. (Premise)
7. Therefore, GOD exists in the understanding. (From 1 and 2)
8. Therefore, GOD exists only in the understanding or in the understanding and in reality. (From 6 and 7)
9. Therefore, GOD can be conceived to exist in reality. (From 3 and 7)
10. Therefore, if GOD exists only in the understanding, then it is possible to conceive of something greater than GOD. (From 4 and 9)

11. Therefore, GOD does not exist only in the understanding. (From 5 and 10)
12. Therefore – drum roll! – GOD exists in reality. (From 8 and 10)

I have framed Anselm's argument so that the premises are up-front, but here is Oppy's way of doing it so that the reasoning is easier to follow:

1. Whatever is understood exists in the understanding. (Premise)
2. The words that-than-which-no-greater-can-be-conceived are understood. (Premise)
3. (Therefore) That-than-which-no-greater-can-be-conceived exists in the understanding. (From 1 and 2)
4. If that-than-which-no-greater-can-be-conceived exists only in the understanding, then that-than-which-no-greater-can-be-conceived-and-that-exists-in-reality is greater than that-than-which-no-greater-can-be-conceived. (Premise)
5. It is impossible for anything to be greater than that-than-which-no-greater-can-be-conceived. (Premise)
6. (Therefore) That-than-which-no-greater-can-be-conceived does not exist only in the understanding. (From 4 and 5)
7. (Therefore) That-than-which-no-greater-can-be-conceived exists in reality. (From 3 and 6) (Oppy 2018: 9)

While there are fewer premises in Oppy's formulation, we would have to spend a little more time explaining the difference between his "that-than-which-no-greater-can-be-conceived" versus "that-than-which-no-greater-can-be-conceived-and-that-exists-in-reality." The argument is also often framed as a

- *reductio ad absurdum*: reasoning that shows that an original assumption results in a contradiction or absurdity, and so must be false.

From the premise that GOD does not exist in reality, derive the absurdity that GOD is not GOD, that something greater than that than which a greater *cannot* be conceived *can* be conceived. Conclude that the original premise that landed us in this absurdity is false and that, therefore, GOD exists in reality (compare Nagasawa 2017: 154–55; see Campbell 2018 for a reconstruction with about *220* premises).

In any case, the objections considered below apply to arguments close enough to the passage to count as an interpretation of Anselm's argument. We will explore an alternative formulation later (see Section 2.10).

2.3 Premises

But first we can explore a little more about the meaning of the premises (focusing on the premises in my own formulation). Premise 1 of my formulation captures

Anselm here: "But when this same fool hears me say 'something than which nothing greater can be thought,'" he surely understand what he hears." Even the fool understands what "GOD" means. The fool must understand what "GOD" means in order to deny the existence of GOD. Compare this to the idea that we must understand what "fairy" means in order to deny the existence of fairies.

The next premise is trickier. Premise 2 is a safer instance of Anselm's "whatever is understood exists in the understanding." At the ellipsis in my quote of the argument, Anselm provides this illustration of what it is to exist in the understanding:

> When a painter, for example, thinks out in advance what he is going to paint, he has it in his understanding, but he does not yet understand that it exists, since he has not yet painted it. But once he has painted it, he both has it in his understanding and understands that it exists because he has now painted it. (1995: 7)

Anselm takes the painting to exist, at first, in the painter's understanding and not in reality. Later, it exists in reality as well as in the understanding. The idea, then, is that there are different ways for the painting to exist: in the understanding or in reality or both. GOD similarly might exist in the understanding or in reality or both. But what exactly Anselm has in mind by existence in the understanding is tricky, as we will see (in Section 2.6).

Premises 3 and 4 capture Anselm's "if it exists only in the understanding, it can be thought to exist in reality as well, which is greater." These premises tell us that GOD might have either kind of existence or both and that one kind is better than the other. This assumes that beings can differ in greatness. But there are different kinds of greatness. Nagasawa (2017: 55) distinguishes among

- greatness for oneself (e.g., the criminal's smarts are great for himself),
- greatness for the world (e.g., the inventor's smarts are great for others),
- greatness in capacity (e.g., the sharpness is great for the knife), and
- intrinsic greatness (e.g., knowledge, power, and goodness make anything great).

What kind of greatness does Anselm have in mind? Being as sharp as a knife is certainly not a relevant property adding to GOD's greatness. The rest of the *Proslogion* spells out GOD's greatness in terms of knowledge, power, and goodness. Anselm has in mind intrinsic greatness, and premise 4 tells us that GOD's existence in reality would add to GOD's intrinsic greatness.

Finally, premise 5 captures Anselm's "that is clearly impossible." If a being is "that than which a greater *cannot* be thought" and yet also such that "a greater *can* be thought," then the being is at once the greatest that can be thought and not the greatest that can be thought – which is a contradiction and thus impossible.

We now turn to objections against the premises in order, as well as against the inferences from them to the conclusion, and against the argument as a whole. Working through the objections also helps towards understanding the premises.

2.4 Understanding

Against premises 1 and 2, the critic might object that "GOD" is not understood and that GOD does not exist in the understanding. The first critic of Anselm's argument – Gaunilo of Marmoutiers, who liked the rest of the *Proslogion* very much – *seems* to target what we have as premise 1. Gaunilo objects:

> When I hear someone speak of that which is greater than everything else that can be thought ... I can no more think of it or have it in my understanding in terms of anything whose genus or species I already know, than I can think of God himself. ... For I do not know the thing itself, and I cannot form an idea of it on the basis of something like it, since you yourself claim that it is so great that nothing else could be like it. Now if I heard something said about a man I do not know at all, whose very existence is unknown to me, I could think of him in accordance with that very thing that a man is, on the basis of that knowledge of the genus or species by which I know what a man is or what men are. (1995: 30)

The passage is obscure, but the idea seems to be that we cannot understand "GOD." We can understand things – including things that we have never seen or that we deny exist – in terms of the familiar kinds they belong to. I can even understand what "centaur" means via my understanding of more familiar things (a horse, a man). However, when it comes to "GOD," there is nothing that we can similarly draw upon. There is just a word: "In the case of God, I can think of him solely on the basis of the word; and one can seldom or never think of any true thing solely on the basis of a word" (1995: 30).

Anselm replies:

> I, however, say this: if that than which a greater cannot be thought is neither understood nor thought, and exists neither in the understanding nor in thought, then either God is not that than which a greater cannot be thought, or else he is neither understood nor thought, and exists neither in the understanding nor in thought. I appeal to your own faith and conscience as the most compelling argument that this is false. Therefore, that than which a greater cannot be thought is indeed understood and thought, and exists in the understanding and thought. (1995: 36)

The reply appeals to Gaunilo's religious belief. Gaunilo understands what "GOD" means insofar as he understands what "God" means, and he does understand the latter as a devout Christian. Gaunilo need only check within to see what we're talking about.

There is a theological tradition about divine transcendence and incomprehensibility. Would this tradition mean that we cannot understand "GOD" and that the ontological argument flops at the get-go? I do not think so. It does mean that we cannot understand a lot about GOD. But we might still understand enough for the argument to get off the ground. Indeed, Anselm also thinks that we cannot know the inner texture of the divine nature. He writes that GOD is "something greater than can be thought" and that GOD is like a blinding light, "too dazzling; my understanding does not grasp it, and the eye of my soul cannot bear to look into it for long" (1995: 17). Nevertheless, we can know *something* about GOD as "that than which a greater cannot be conceived," and that is what the ontological argument depends on.

2.5 Meinong

The next premise is especially tricky. Premise 3 makes a distinction between existence in reality (Latin: *in re*) versus existence in the understanding (Latin: *in solo intellectu*). Distinguish easily enough between

- existence in the external world (for example, the *Mona Lisa* hangs in the Louvre); and
- existence in the mental world (for example, your idea–or mental image or concept–of the *Mona Lisa* with a cat on her lap hangs in your mind's eye, not in the Louvre).

Commentators tell us that the distinction between existence *in re* and existence *in solo intellectu* is *not* the distinction between existence in the external world and existence in the mental world (see van Inwagen 2012: 147–8). Both the external world and the mental world are *in re*; they are just different *parts* of reality.

Distinguish then between existence in reality (whether in the external world or the mental world) and

- a degraded realm of being, or what Alexius Meinong (1853–1920) calls *subsistence*.

The idea is that there are some things that do not exist but subsist: nonexistent objects living in a metaphysical shadow realm. This means that "there are" and "exists" do not mean the same thing. The *Mona Lisa* exists. The *idea* of the *Mona Lisa* with a cat on her lap exists too. But the

Mona Lisa with the cat on her lap does not exist. Here are some other examples of things that exist:

- Queen Elizabeth II,
- the moon, and
- a book by Sir Arthur Conan Doyle.

And examples of things that do not exist:

- the present King of France,
- Pegasus, and
- Sherlock Holmes.

Peter van Inwagen takes Anselm's argument to endorse the following:

> *Meinongian Existence Thesis*: That even if the Fool is right when he says that something than which nothing greater can be conceived does not exist in reality, it remains true that the phrase "something than which nothing greater can be conceived" denotes a certain item – an item that enjoys a weaker, less demanding mode of existence than existence in reality, to wit, existence *in intellectu*. (2012: 150)

Here, "a less demanding mode of existence" refers to what we call *subsistence*. The idea is that at the beginning of the argument, we know that GOD at least has subsistence (from premises 1 and 2). But that if GOD has subsistence, then he might have existence (premise 3), and GOD is greater if he has existence (premise 4), and so on.

Van Inwagen demurs that "Meinongianism in any form is simply wrong" (2012: 151). We cannot cover the big debate over being, but the next section briefly surveys some of the arguments for Meinongianism. Curiously, Meinong himself did not accept the ontological argument (see Marek 2019).

2.6 Nonexistent

What motivates the dark doctrine of Meinongianism? At least four related ideas (see Reicher 2019). The first is about

- intentionality. Meinong had a *principle of intentionality* that psychological states are about things. To love is to love something, to fear is to fear something, and so on. But people often love and fear things that do not exist, like false gods and monsters. Meinong concluded that *there are* some things that do not *exist* but instead subsist.

The next three ideas are about truthmakers for sentences about nonexistent objects – at least my preferred way of framing them is in terms of *truthmakers*.

Generally, sentences are made true by their parts referring to objects in the right arrangement. For example, "the cat is on the mat" is made true by the cat, the mat, and their positions. But there are true sentences

- explicitly about nonexistent things. "Pegasus does not exist" must be made true, in part, by Pegasus. But Pegasus, as the sentence tells us explicitly, does not exist. There are some things, then, that do not exist but instead subsist.

Then there are sentences less explicitly about nonexistent things. There are true sentences about

- fictional things. The sentence "Harry Potter is a wizard" is true. Again, there must be something that makes it true: Harry Potter. This time round, the sentence does not say that Harry Potter does not exist, but he does not (unless *realism* about fictional characters is true; see Thomasson 1998). There are some things, then, that do not exist but instead subsist.

Finally, there are true sentences about

- the past. The sentence "Meinong was a philosopher" is true. Again, there must be something that makes it true: Meinong. While Meinong once existed, he no longer exists (or if his soul does, consider his *body* instead). There are some things, then, that do not exist but instead subsist.

The same kind of problem can be generated for sentences about the future, about things that do not exist but will – all the problems depending on certain views of time. The ideas in each of the four cases above are quite similar. But slight differences make general replies tricky. For example, an opponent could reply that the fictional sentence "Harry Potter is a wizard" is simply not true. But the opponent could hardly reply that the sentence "Meinong was a philosopher" is not true.

To be sure, even the reply about fictional sentences does not sound right. For there is a difference in truth between

- "Harry Potter is a wizard" and
- "Harry Potter is a helicopter."

But, if they are both equally false, what could that difference be? The opponent can answer by distinguishing between

- truth simpliciter: where both sentences are equally false; and
- truth in the fiction: where the first sentence is true, but the second is false.

The answer proposes that sentences about fictional objects are only true when prefaced by "In the story of *Harry Potter*," or "In the story of *Macbeth*," and so on. This strategy faces its own problems, however. Consider the following sentence:

- Harry Potter is the main character of J. K. Rowling's series.

That sentence is about a fictional object and it is true. But it is not true when prefaced by "In the story of *Harry Potter*." The sentence is not true in the fiction: J. K. Rowling and her series do not feature within the story at all. The sentence is a true simpliciter. The opponent will have to find a different truthmaker for the sentence then – one that does not involve Harry Potter.

Maybe this can be done. And maybe similar strategies can be developed to deal with intentionality, nonexistent objects, and the past. Or maybe other strategies can be developed. Or maybe not (see Miravalle 2018). And then there are *objections* directly against Meinongianism, not merely against the arguments for Meinongianism (see van Inwagen 2001). For example, there are objections about:

- the obscurity of the doctrine: Do we really understand existence versus subsistence?
- the determinacy of nonexistent objects: How many sisters would Sherlock Holmes have?
- harboring contradictions (see Russell 1905): Can the round square (the alleged truthmaker for "the round square is round") really have any being?

And there are replies to those objections, and elaborations of Meinongianism and neo-Meinongianism (see, e.g., Parsons 1980). Things become tricky quickly. Meinongianism is no easy business. What I have presented is more how Meinong has been received (by some) than his own view. There is the joke (attributed to Shalom Rosenberg of the Hebrew University) about rival inter-pretations of the medieval Jewish philosopher Maimonides (1135–1204), including Guttman's Maimonides, Pines's Maimonides, Strauss's Maimonides, Wolfson's Maimonides, and then *my*-monides. Similarly, there might be Meinong, and my-nong and your-nong.

2.7 Nihilism

The argument is also threatened by nihilism about value: the view that there is no such thing as intrinsic greatness. If there is no such thing as intrinsic greatness, then GOD is not *really* greater for existing in reality than for existing only in the understanding, and premise 4 is false.

Nihilists would have to deny the existence of God – at least if the divine attributes would mean that there is value or intrinsic greatness. Plausibly, omnibenevolence would mean that there is. Some other arguments for the existence of God get some mileage, independently of a commitment to value;

for example, cosmological arguments pointing to the beginning of the universe make no assumption about value, at least not so explicitly. That the ontological argument does depend on such an assumption is a weak spot.

A related worry is that our values are not on target. Daniel Dennett objects that the conclusion of the ontological argument must be pretty bare:

> [T]he price [proponents of the argument] pay (willingly, one gathers) for their access to purely logical proof is a remarkably bare and featureless intentional object. Even if a *Being greater than which nothing can be conceived* has to exist, as their arguments urge, it is a long haul from that specification to a Being that is merciful or just or loving – unless you make sure to define it that way from the outset, introducing anthropomorphism by a dodge that will not persuade the skeptics, needless to say. Nor – in my experience – does it reassure the faithful. (2006: 242)

Even if the ontological argument proves that there is a greatest conceivable or perfect being, we still have to determine what *greatest* or *perfect* mean. That determination will be in terms of values, but who is to say that *our* values track real value, "whatever it is better to be than not to be," as Anselm puts it? This objection is not so much a nihilism about the reality of value as a skepticism about our knowledge of it: even if there is such a thing as intrinsic greatness, we have no reliable way of telling what it is.

Critics do not usually object against ontological arguments on the basis of nihilism or skepticism about value, since such nihilism and skepticism are themselves controversial and unpopular. Still, they are popular enough for the problem to be noted (see Streumer 2018; Street 2006; and Huemer 2005, in the opposite direction).

2.8 Parody

Gaunilo presents a few objections against the ontological argument. We discussed one already (see Section 2.4). But his most famous objection is a *parody* of the argument, an ontological argument for the existence of an island:

> This island (so the story goes) is more plentifully endowed than even the Isles of the Blessed with an indescribable abundance of all sorts of riches and delights. .... Suppose someone tells me all this. The story is easily told and involves no difficulty, and so I understand it. But if this person went on to draw a conclusion, and say, "You cannot any longer doubt that this island, more excellent than all others on earth, truly exists somewhere in reality. For you do not doubt that this island exists in your understanding, and since it is more excellent to exist not merely in the understanding, but also in reality, this island must also exist in reality. For if it did not, any land that exists in reality would be greater than it. And so this more excellent thing that you have

understood would not in fact be more excellent." – If, I say, he should try to convince me by this argument that I should no longer doubt whether the island truly exists, either I would think he was joking, or I would not know whom I ought to think more foolish: myself, if I grant his conclusion, or him. (1995: 31–32)

The parody simply substitutes "island than which no greater can be conceived" for "something than which no greater can be conceived." So far as the argument we have framed above goes, abbreviate "island than which no greater can be conceived" with *ISLAND* and substitute *ISLAND* for *GOD*. The conclusion is then that ISLAND exists in reality. ISLAND would presumably have crystal beaches, ripe coconuts, and chocolate volcanos.

Since the arguments are so similar, if the ontological argument works, then the island argument works. But the island argument must go wrong; there are no chocolate volcanos. So the ontological argument must go wrong too. The objection does not identify where exactly the wrong premise or inference is. There is a whole cottage industry of parodies against the ontological argument, including "devil" parodies for and against the existence of a being than which a worse cannot be conceived – which, depending on how the parodies go,

- cannot exist, since not existing is worse than existing; or
- must exist, since it would be worse (could do more evil) by existing than not existing (for treatment of these, see Chambers 2000; Nagasawa 2017: chapter 6).

As we will see, parodies have also been applied to other ontological arguments.

2.9 Difference

Anselm replies to the parody, but obscurely. The most popular reply is that the ontological argument and the island argument differ in a relevant way. As for "that than which a greater cannot be conceived," there are maximum limits to the features that make a being great. For example, a being cannot be more powerful than omnipotent, more knowledgeable than omniscient, and so forth. Thus "GOD" is understood, and GOD exists in the understanding.

In contrast, there are no maximum limits to the features that make an island great. For example, the addition of another chocolate volcano always makes an island greater. Since a yet greater island can always be thought, "ISLAND" is not understood, and ISLAND does not exist in the understanding. Thus premise 1 of the ontological argument is true, while the corresponding premise of the island argument is not. As Plantinga puts it:

The idea of an island than which it's not possible that there be a greater is like the idea of a natural number than which it's not possible that there be a greater. ... The qualities that make for greatness in an island – number of palm trees, amount and quality of coconuts, for example – most of these qualities have no *intrinsic maximum*.

In contrast:

Knowledge, for example, does have an intrinsic maximum: if for every proposition *p*, a being *B* knows whether or not *p* is true, then *B* has a degree of knowledge that is utterly unsurpassable. So a greatest possible being would have to have this kind of knowledge: it would have to be *omniscient*. Similarly for *power*; omnipotence is a degree of power that can't possibly be excelled. Moral perfection or moral excellence is perhaps not quite so clear; still a being could perhaps always do what is morally right, so that it would not be possible for it to be exceeded along those lines. (1974: 90–91)

The answer is problematic from both sides. As for GOD, the problem is that while there are maximum limits for some features that make GOD great, there might not be for other such features. For example, GOD might always be more good – by doing another good action. Plantinga notes that when it comes to whether love has an intrinsic maximum, "there might be a weak point here in Anselm's argument" (1974: 91; also see Conee 2013: 115). As for ISLAND, while there are no maximum limits for some features that make ISLAND great, there might be for other such features. For example, such features as having *any* chocolate volcanos.

Such problems can be answered. The problem with GOD assumes that a being is made more good by doing more good. But, if a being can always do more good, then there is no maximum good. If so, then it is no moral failure for not doing the maximum good, since there is no moral failure in not doing what cannot be done – *ought* implies *can*. If so, then a being could be maximally good without doing the maximum good. Thus a being is not necessarily made more good by doing more good.

Another answer denies that GOD could always do another good action: perhaps GOD has already created an infinite multiverse of good universes. Some argue that GOD has (see Kraay 2010), and it is hard to see how much real evidence there could be against the hypothesis – apart from evidence that *ours* is not a good enough universe.

2.10 Millican

Peter Millican (2004) discovers what he takes to be "a fatal flaw" in Anselm's argument. The flaw would be a relatively superficial logical mistake, and the objection is supposed to be superior to previous objections since it does not rely on any controversial metaphysical assumptions against the argument (see Millican 2004: 470).

Millican frames the argument and the objection in terms of

- natures: bundles of properties

that may or may not be *instantiated* or had. For example, the nature <Aurelius> is the bundle of wisdom, justice, being emperor of Rome, and so on, and was instantiated (Marcus Aurelius had it). The nature <Arthur> is the bundle of saintliness, heroism, being king of England, and so on, and, we suppose, was never instantiated. The nature <God> is the bundle of omnipotence, omniscience, and omnibenevolence, and the argument tries to prove that this nature is instantiated, as follows:

1. The phrase "a-nature-than-which-no-greater-nature-can-be-thought" is clearly understood by the fool, and apparently makes sense.
2. Hence we can take the phrase "a-nature-than-which-no-greater-nature-can-be-thought" as successfully denoting some specific nature.
3. A nature that is instantiated in reality is greater than one which is not.
4. So if a-nature-than-which-no-greater-nature-can-be-thought were not instantiated in reality, then it would be possible to think of a nature that is greater (for example, any nature that is in fact instantiated in reality).
5. But this would be a contradiction, since it is obviously impossible to think of a nature that is greater than a-nature-than-which-no-greater-nature-can-be-thought.
6. Therefore a-nature-than-which-no-greater-nature-can-be-thought must indeed be instantiated in reality (2004: 457–58; numbering reformatted).

Framing the argument in terms of instantiated versus uninstantiated natures instead of existent versus nonexistent beings avoids the question about Meinongianism. To be sure, the distinction between instantiated versus uninstantiated properties also raises questions:

> for this strategy to work the *existence of the nature itself* . . . must be clearly distinguished from that nature's *instantiation*. . . . If this distinction is not drawn, then the argument is hopeless: the atheist can simply point out that [premise 2] begs the question by purporting to make reference to something whose existence he denies. (Millican 2007: 1044)

But the distinction between instantiated versus uninstantiated properties is much less controversial than the distinction between existence versus subsistence. Millican's formulation is supposed to bypass various other objections leveled against Anselm besides (see Millican 2004: 458–59), and thus to be an optimal version of the argument. And yet, Millican argues, the argument fails upon disambiguating the meaning of "nature-than-which-no-greater-nature-can-be-thought." The meaning will depend on whether the nature <God> is supposed to be

- in fact greater, or
- thought of as greater,

and whether other natures are supposed to be

- in fact less great, or
- thought of as less great.

Altogether then the "nature-than-which-no-greater-nature-can-be-thought" can have four meanings. First, it might mean

- a nature that *is* so great no nature *is* greater.

The audience might take the nature to be <God> or e.g. <Aurelius>. If they think <God> is instantiated, then they will take the nature to be <God>. But, if not, they might take it to be <Aurelius>. Thus they might accept that the argument is sound, but that the conclusion is about <Aurelius>, not <God>.

Second, the phrase might mean

- a nature that *can be thought* so great that no nature *can be thought* greater.

Now the audience might take the nature to be <God>; they might imagine <God> as the greatest instantiated nature. But imagining does not make it so. Instead, they might deny that <God> is instantiated, and thus deny premise 5 that it is impossible to think of a greater nature. For, in light of premise 3 that an instantiated nature is greater than an uninstantiated nature, if <God> is not instantiated, then <Aurelius> will be thought greater than <God>.

Third, the phrase might mean

- a nature that *is* so great that no nature *can be thought* greater.

Now the audience might not take there to be such a nature. They might deny premise 2 that the relevant phrase names anything at all. They might deny premise 1 too, or the move from premise 1 to premise 2.

Finally, the phrase might mean:

- a nature that *can be thought* so great that no nature *is* greater.

Now the audience might take the nature to be <God> or <Aurelius>, depending on which they think is instantiated. They might imagine either as the greatest nature. But imagining does not make it so. If <God> is instantiated, then no nature is greater. But, again, they might deny that <God> is instantiated, and thus deny premise 5. For, in light of premise 3, if <God> is not instantiated, <Aurelius> would be thought greater than <God>.

On each reading, the audience can easily reject the argument, at least as an argument for the existence of God (see Millican 2004: 463–67; 2007: 1047–48). Millican takes the moral to generalize against other ontological arguments, including Descartes's and Plantinga's (though he does not apply it to other ontological arguments treated below).

We can slip Aquinas's objection against Anselm in here, since it *might* be close to Millican's. But the idea is opaque:

> even if it is granted that everyone understands the name "God" to signify . . . "that than which a greater cannot be thought" . . . nevertheless it does not follow from this that one understands that what is signified by the name exists in the natural order, but rather only in the apprehension of the intellect. Nor can it be argued that it exists in reality unless it were granted that there exists in reality something than which a greater cannot be thought, which would not be granted by those who deny that God exists. (Aquinas 2014: 51)

As on Millican's interpretations, Aquinas objects to Anselm's idea that one who denies that God exists is entangled in a contradiction. Among the historical objections, Millican takes only Aquinas's as "relatively clearly on target" (2004: 466) insofar as it blocks the move from premise 4 to premise 5 (see Leftow 2018 for more on Aquinas's objection).

2.11 Optimal

Nagasawa (2017; 2007) takes Millican's formulation to be suboptimal. Premise 3 states what Nagasawa calls

> The principle of the superiority of existence: Any nature that is instantiated is greater than any nature that is not instantiated (or any nature that is conceived only in the mind). (2017: 136)

But he argues that Anselm neither endorses nor requires this premise. Instead, Nagasawa proposes replacing premise 3 with:

> 3'. A-nature-than-which-no-greater-nature-can-be-thought that is instantiated in reality is greater than a-nature-than-which-no-greater-nature-can-be-thought that is conceived only in the mind (because existence is a great-making property). (Nagasawa 2017: 144; numbering reformatted)

And accordingly replacing premise 4 with:

> 4'. So if a-nature-than-which-no-greater-nature-can-be-thought were not instantiated in reality, then it would be possible to think of a nature that is greater; namely, a-nature-than-which-no-greater-nature-can-be-thought that is instantiated in reality. (2017: 144; numbering reformatted)

Take the second interpretation of "nature-than-which-no-greater-nature-can-be-thought" as a nature that *can be thought* so great that no *nature can be thought greater*. Previously, the audience could deny premise 5 in light of premise 3 or the principle of the superiority of existence. But the new premise 3' will not allow for this. Thus the conclusion is reached less problematically.

2.12 Suboptimal

Millican (2007) replies that Nagasawa's formulation falls into the same old trap, and Nagasawa (2017: 148–49) replies in turn that whether it does depends on just the kind of controversial metaphysical principle Millican's formulation is supposed to bypass.

Instead of adjudicating their debate, here's a simpler objection from Earl Conee (2013) that would count against both Millican's and Nagasawa's formulations. Their formulations assume that <God> is a-nature-than-which-no-greater-nature-can-be-thought. While God would be the greatest being in virtue of *having* omnipotence, omniscience, and omnibenevolence, that does not mean that <God> is great in virtue of being *composed of* omnipotence, omniscience, and omnibenevolence. The premises assume that the *natures* have a greatness corresponding to the *beings* having that natures. But this is not obvious. Conee has an alternative proposal:

> The greatness of a nature seems rather to be determined by whatever enhances the magnificence of an abstract object that is composed of properties. Perhaps this enhancement is affected by the great quantity of the properties that compose it, or by their great diversity, or by the intricacy of the logical relationships among them. (2013: 114)

Conee presents what he takes to be an optimal formulation of Anselm's argument instead:

1. An absolutely greatest being is conceivable.
2. An absolutely greatest being that exists is absolutely greater than is an absolutely greatest being that does not exist.
3. Therefore, if an absolutely greatest being does not exist, then it is possible for a conceivable being to be absolutely greater than an absolutely greatest being.
4. It is not possible for a conceivable being to be absolutely greater than an absolutely greatest being.
5. Therefore, an absolutely greatest being does exist. (Conee 2013: 118, renumbered and edited slightly)

Conee proceeds to reject this argument. But he tells us that the argument is not hostage to Meinongianism. Premise 2 is supposed to be "nearly rationally irresistible" (2013: 120). And it is if Meinongianism is true:

> If no absolutely greatest being exists, then at most there is some nonexistent Meinongian object that somehow qualifies as an absolutely greatest being. The nonexistent being is omniscient in just the way that the Meinongian nonexistent gold mountain is a mountain made out of gold. Whatever that way of being made out of gold is, it does not excite prospectors. Gold that exists is way better. Similarly, a defender of [premise 2] can quite reasonably contend that genuinely existing with great properties like omniscience is a greater way to be. So if some absolutely greatest being is real but nonexistent, then [premise 2] is right that an existing absolutely greatest being would be absolutely greater. (2013: 120)

But Conee takes the premise to remain plausible even if

> we set Meinongianism aside. Suppose that there is no absolutely greatest being with any kind of reality, if one does not exist. Instead, when we reflect on the idea of a GCB [greatest conceivable being], we are just conceiving of how such a thing would be. This conception has no object at all, and so none that is any actual good. In contrast, the real thing would be terrifically great. Clearly, the real thing would be absolutely greater than its absence. So [premise 2] is acceptable, with or without nonexistent objects. (2013: 120–21)

And he might be right about the premise: God would be greater than his *absence*. But in the *absence* of Meinongianism, the rest of the argument will not go through. If premise 2 is about an absence, then premise 3 must be about an absence too: if there is no greatest conceivable being, then it is possible for a conceivable being to be greater than some absence. And then premise 4 is about an absence too: it's not possible for a conceivable being to be greater than some absence. But that's not plausible. Without Meinongianism, there is an absence of hope for anything like Conee's formulation (for yet other formulations, with criticisms, see Barnes 1972; Lewis 1970).

2.13 Conclusion

Anselm's argument depends on various controversial moral and metaphysical principles. Nagasawa points out that

> dispute over the classical ontological argument for perfect being theism endures even nine centuries after Anselm introduced it because the argument is structured in such a way that one cannot refute it without making a significant metaphysical or epistemic assumption that is likely to be contentious in its own right. That is, there is no uncontroversial, straightforward

refutation of the argument that would convince a majority of its defenders to concede that it does not succeed. (2017: 152)

We have just begun to discover this insight. But the point cuts both ways. Just as

- the success of the objection to Anselm's argument depends on, for example, Meinongianism turning out false,
- the success of the argument depends on Meinongianism turning out true.

Since Meinongianism is not an easy question, both an easy refutation and an easy defense of the argument are ruled out. Nagasawa concludes that proponents and opponents of Anselm's argument "end in a draw" (2017: 179).

Yet, where there are many assumptions at work in the argument, there is an asymmetry that puts opponents of the argument in a better position. Their success depends on *any* one of the metaphysical questions turning out the right way for them. One successful objection is enough to sink the argument. But the success of the proponents depends on *all* the metaphysical questions turning out the right way for *them*. Anselm's argument will not persuade anyone who is not a Meinongian *or* does not subscribe to any of the other controversial metaphysical assumptions at work in the argument. Destruction is easier than construction – a general philosophical predicament and a general predicament.

3 Descartes

3.1 Meditation

Let's skip a few centuries from Anselm to Descartes. Descartes presents a couple arguments for the existence of God. His ontological argument is presented in his *Fifth Meditation*:

> But if the mere fact that I can produce from my thought the idea of something entails that everything which I clearly and distinctly perceive to belong to that thing really does belong to it, is not this a possible basis for another argument to prove the existence of God? Certainly, the idea of God, or a supremely perfect being, is one which I find within me just as surely as the idea of any shape or number. And my understanding that it belongs to his nature that he always exists is no less clear and distinct than in the case when I prove of any shape or number that some property belongs to its nature. Hence, even if it turned out that not everything on which I have meditated these past days is true, I ought still to regard the existence of God as having at least the same level of certainty as I have hitherto attributed to the truths of mathematics (1986: 45)

And also in his *Replies* to Johannes Caterus (c. 1590–1655):

> That which we clearly and distinctly understand to belong to the true and immutable nature, or essence, or form of something, can be truly asserted of

that thing. But once we have made a sufficiently careful investigation of what God is, we clearly and distinctly understand that existence belongs to his true and immutable nature. Hence we can now truly assert of God that he does exist. (1986: 100)

And in other places besides. Each presentation is slightly different, and what exactly Descartes has in mind is open to interpretation. Indeed, Lawrence Nolan (2018) argues – much more plausibly than Barth does on Anselm – that Descartes does not really mean to endorse a line of reasoning so much as to dress up as such a kind of immediate intellectual insight that God must exist. But, since I have a book to write, I will consider Descartes's argument as most others have.

3.2 Interpretation

Descartes's argument is often put in terms of the "definition" of a perfect being (see, e.g., Lowe 2013):

1. A perfect being, by definition, has every perfection.
2. Existence is a perfection.
3. Therefore, a perfect being has existence (i.e., exists).

This reconstruction leaves out Descartes's ideas about what we "clearly and distinctly" understand, apprehend or perceive. Georges Dicker has a closer version:

1. Whatever I clearly and distinctly perceive to belong to the nature or essence of a thing does belong to its nature or essence.
2. Whatever belongs to the nature or essence of a thing can be truly affirmed of that thing.
3. Therefore, whatever I clearly and distinctly perceive to belong to the nature or essence of a thing can be truly affirmed of that thing.
4. I clearly and distinctly perceive that existence belongs to the nature or essence of a supremely perfect being.
5. Therefore, existence can be truly affirmed of a supremely perfect being (i.e., a supremely perfect being exists). (2013: 223–4; renumbered and reorganized slightly)

There are yet other formulations (see, e.g., Naylor van Inwagen 1969; Stang 2016: 44–49). But usually the arguments are something like one of the above, and I will refer back to each as the

- *simple reconstruction*, and
- *elaborate reconstruction*

respectively. What exactly Descartes means by *clarity* and *distinctness* and why he takes them to be a mark of truth would entangle us in other parts of his *Meditations* (see Wilson 2003: 80–85). So our critique focuses on different parts of his argument.

Ontological arguments close to Descartes's – especially in the simple reconstruction – are put forward by, for example, Baruch Spinoza (1631–77):

> If you deny [that God necessarily exists], conceive, if you can, that God does not exist. Therefore (Ax.7) his essence does not involve existence. But this is absurd (Pr.7). Therefore God necessarily exists. (1992: 37)

And Mary Astell (1666–1731):

> Existence is a Perfection, and the Foundation of all other Perfections, since that which has no Being cannot be suppos'd to have any Perfection. And tho the Idea of Existence is not Adequate to that of Perfection, yet the Idea of Perfection Includes that of Existence, and if *That* Idea were divided into parts, one part of it wou'd exactly agree with *This*. So that if we will allow that *Any* Being is Infinite in All Perfections, we cannot deny that that Being Exists; Existence it self being one Perfection, and such an one as all the rest are built upon. (2002: 180)

Among others. The critique of Descartes easily applies to these other arguments too.

3.3 Déjà vu

Some of the debate over Anselm's argument applies against Descartes's too. The argument can be parodied in a similar way. Substitute "perfect island" for "perfect being," and then the conclusion is that there must exist an island with crystal beaches, ripe coconuts, and chocolate volcanos. The objection again does not identify where exactly the wrong premise or inference is.

Following the reply to the parody of Anselm's argument, the natural response is to deny that there is any relevant idea of a perfect island. The reply targets the parody at the

- first premise in the simple reconstruction: the premise assumes that there could be a perfect island; and
- fourth premise in the elaborate reconstruction: the premise assumes that there is an essence of a perfect island.

The point is familiar: an additional chocolate volcano will always make for the idea of a better island, so that there could not be a perfect island or an essence of a perfect island. So while the premise of Descartes's argument is true, the premise of the parody is false. Rinse, wash, and repeat the treatment of the parody above.

3.4 Existence

And some of the debate over Descartes's argument applies against Anselm too. Both Anselm and Descartes seem to take existence to be a great-making feature of a thing–in

- premise 4 of Anselm's argument (see Section 2.2),
- premise 2 of the simpler reconstruction, and
- premise 4 of the elaborate reconstruction of Descartes.

Critics might question whether existence is a perfection. I could have presented this point earlier about Anselm's argument – but keeping you on your toes.

John-Mark Miravalle replies that asking whether existence is a perfection is like

> asking what makes movies in full color better than movies in black and white, given that the movies in black and white are just as detailed as the color films. One could only answer that the color makes everything richer, more brilliant. ... Things that are real matter – whatever goodness they possess is made worthwhile, important, not to be neglected – because they exist. Things are better when they exist. (2018: 81)

To be sure, movies in black and white are not as detailed as the color ones: color gives detail. But, then again, existence gives something too: nonexisting things cannot do very much at all.

The critic might press with counterexamples against the general rule: "things like sickness or death or mortgage – which seem to be better precisely when they don't exist" (Miravalle 2018: 81). Here existence is no perfection or great-making property at all; on the contrary, in the case of suffering or wickedness existence is an imperfection or worse-making quality. Existence might make them greater *in a sense*, but not in the sense of making them better – in the sense of making them worse.

Miravalle replies in two ways. First, that what is bad about suffering and wickedness is not their existence, so much as the nonexistence of other things:

> What is responsible for our repugnance in these cases is not so much the fact that certain things exist as the fact that certain other things don't. "Getting rid of sickness" is simply an idiom for trying to restore health, delaying death means prolonging life. ... In other words, overcoming evil always involves trying to bring about or maintain the existence of other things, and this seems to support the idea of existence as an unqualified good. (2018: 81–2)

On the medieval view of *evil as a privation*, suffering and wickedness do not exist at all, not strictly speaking. They are just the absences of something good – sickness is the absence of health, death is the absence of life, etc. – assuming that *absences* do not really exist. If suffering and wickedness do not ever exist, then existence is not what makes them worse. But the idea is problematic, since we might wonder whether suffering and wickedness are just absences and whether absences do not really exist. Hence Miravalle's second answer, framed re Anselm's argument:

> Anselm never claims that existence is a perfection generally, or that anything automatically becomes better just by existing. All Anselm says (roughly) is that what is unqualifiedly perfect is better if it exists, and this more modest principle seems much less open to controversy. Certainly it's more plausible to say that something good, especially something unqualifiedly good, is better when it exists. It's good for good to exist, and if it's good for good to exist, then it's good for the most good (i.e. perfection) to exist. (2018: 82)

The main point applies to Descartes's argument too, whatever he would claim about existence generally. We could make it explicit by framing premise 2 a little differently, as, for example: existence is a perfection *for a perfect being*; or existence is a perfection *except for evil beings*.

3.5 Lions

Descartes's argument and ontological arguments more generally are often accused of trying to "define things into existence." This is especially the case with the simpler reconstruction, where premise 1 defines a *perfect being*. Caterus plays around with the definition of an *existing lion*:

> The complex "existing lion" includes both "lion" and "existence," and it includes them essentially, for if you take away either element it will not be the same complex. . . . And does not the idea of the composite, as a composite, involve both elements essentially? In other words, does not existence belong to the essence of the composite "existing lion"? (1986: 99)

Since there actually are lions, we might do better to put the objection in terms of an *existing unicorn*. Anyhow, just as we do not accept any such proof of a lion, so too

> even if I have distinct knowledge of a supremely perfect being, and even if the supremely perfect being includes existence as an essential part of the concept, it still does not follow that the existence in question is anything actual. (1986: 99)

If we can prove that a perfect being exists via some definition, then we can prove that just about anything exists (a lion, a unicorn) via an appropriate definition (of an *existing lion*, an *existing unicorn*). The point is similar to the parody: since we reject the proof of the lion or unicorn, so too must we reject the proof of the perfect being.

Descartes replies to Caterus by pointing out a big difference between the existing lion and the perfect being. The idea of the existing lion brings together ideas (of existence, of a lion) which can be separated in thought too:

> [W]e must notice a point about ideas which do not contain true and immut-able natures but merely ones which are invented and put together by the intellect. Such ideas can always be split up by the same intellect. . . . When, for example, I think of a winged horse or an actually existing lion . . . I am readily able to think of a horse without wings, or a lion which does not exist. (1986: 100–101)

In contrast, the idea of a perfect being does not bring together separable ideas (e.g., of power, of existence). While at first we might think that the ideas are separable, when we look more carefully into them, we discover that they are not:

> [W]hen we attend to the immense power of [a perfect] being, we shall be unable to think of its existence as possible without also recognizing that it can exist by its own power; and we shall infer from this that this being does really exist and has existed from eternity, since it is quite evident by the natural light that what can exist by its own power always exists. So shall we come to understand that necessary existence is contained in the idea of a supremely perfect being, not by any fiction of the intellect, but because it belongs to the true and immutable nature of such a being that it exists. (1986: 102)

Two questions about Descartes's response: First, is he right that the ideas of, for example, perfect power and existence are inseparable? Second, does this make a relevant difference? While he has a little argument for the inseparability, Descartes does not try to show that separability matters.

The same point applies to other attempts to identify some difference between the ideas of the existing lion, et al., and of the perfect being. For example, Miravalle notes the following:

> The parodies are all generated by verbally joining multiplied words or concepts that proponents of the ontological argument can claim do not refer to things joined in fact: a perfect island, an existent unicorn, or a necessarily existing imperfect thing. By contrast, the ontological argument highlights the referent of a single word, "perfect," and contends that reflection on the referent of that word yields the insight that what doesn't exist is less than perfect and so what is perfect can't be what doesn't exist. Therefore, what is perfect exists. (2018: 83)

And Lowe draws the distinction between *real* definitions versus *purely verbal* definitions, where only *real* definition gets at the nature or essence things. For example, the definition

- "a bachelor is an unmarried man" is a purely verbal definition, telling us only how to use a world, and not about the fundamental, inner texture of anything, whereas
- "a circle is a closed line all of whose points are equidistant from a certain point" is a real definition, telling us something about the fundamental nature of a circle.

The idea is that the parodies do not provide any real definitions, whereas

> according to Anselm, Descartes, and other adherents of the ontological argument, the real definition of God is distinctive and remarkable, in that it tells us that what God is or would be is something that could not fail to exist. And that, in their view, is why we are rationally compelled to conclude that, indeed, he does exist. All we need to come to this conclusion is to grasp the real definition of God, that is, understand what God is or would be. Actually, we do not even need to fully grasp what God is or would be ... but just to grasp that, at the very least, he is or would be a maximally great being. (Lowe 2013: 398)

The question of relevance remains. Miravalle does not show how the number of words or concepts is relevant. And could the critic not simply introduce a single word, e.g., *existinglion* and define it as an existing lion? Lowe does not show how the distinction between real and purely verbal definitions means that the ontological argument works while the parodies fail.

3.6 Hume

Hume presents another general objection against ontological arguments that would apply equally to Descartes and Anselm. Here is as good a place to consider it as any other. It runs as follows:

> I shall begin with observing that there is an evident absurdity in pretending to demonstrate a matter of fact, or to prove it by any arguments *a priori*. Nothing is demonstrable, unless the contrary implies a contradiction. Nothing that is distinctly conceivable implies a contradiction. Whatever we conceive as existent, we can also conceive as non-existent. There is no being, therefore, whose non-existence implies a contradiction. Consequently there is no being whose existence is demonstrable. I propose this argument as entirely decisive, and am willing to rest the whole controversy upon it. (1998: 55)

The idea is that

- if a conclusion can be proved *a priori*, then its denial implies a contradiction;
- if something implies a contradiction, then it is not distinctly conceivable; and
- the denial of the existence of a being is distinctly conceivable.

Putting this all together: since the denial of the existence of a being is distinctly conceivable, it does not imply a contradiction; and since it does not imply a contradiction, the conclusion that such a being exists cannot be proved *a priori*. Applied to the case at hand: the denial of the existence of a perfect being is distinctly conceivable, so it does not imply a contradiction, and so the conclusion that a perfect being exists cannot be proved by an ontological argument. Like Gaunilo's objection against Anselm, the objection does not show where exactly the ontological argument goes wrong – which premise is false, which step is invalid.

But the objection is precarious. Why suppose any of the assumptions true? Hume provides no reason for thinking that if a conclusion can be proved *a priori*, then its denial implies a contradiction; or that if something implies a contradiction, then it is not distinctly conceivable; or that the denial of the existence of a being is distinctly conceivable.

A part of the problem is the difficulty of understanding what Hume means by "conceivable" and "distinctly conceivable." Hume switches between these terms. There might be some sense in which we can "conceive" of the existence as well as the nonexistence of a perfect being: we can at least think about these things. But in that sense, we conceive of all sorts of impossible things: we can think about square circles and the like. Presumably we cannot "distinctly conceive" of such things. Now the question is whether the denial of the existence of a perfect being is distinctly conceivable. We can't picture it (see Swinburne 2012 for a Humean view; and Pruss & Rasmussen 2018: 179–82 for a reply).

3.7 Kant

The most famous objection against Descartes's ontological argument is from Kant. Be forewarned: Kant is a bad writer with complicated ideas. Like everything else in Kant, his objection is open to various interpretations (see Naylor van Inwagen 1969: 62–75; Stang 2015 for detailed treatment). Kant actually has a number of related objections against the ontological argument, but our focus is on a simplified version of his most famous. Here goes:

> *Being* is obviously not a real predicate, i.e., a concept of something that could add to the concept of a thing. It is merely the positing of a thing or of certain determinations in themselves. . . . Now if I take the subject (God) together with all his predicates (among which omnipotence belongs), and say *God is*, or there is a God, then I add no new predicate to the concept of God, but only posit the subject in itself with all its predicates, and indeed posit the *object* in relation to my *concept*. (1998: 567; bold traded for italics)

A *real predicate* is a property – a feature, attribute, or characteristic, like *being red* or *being square*. Imagine a mouse. Now imagine a red mouse. The concept (or idea) of *redness* adds to your mental image. Redness is then a bona fide property. Imagine a mouse. Now imagine an *existing* mouse. Does the concept of existence add anything? The objection is that existence is not like redness; existence is not a property of anything. If existence is not a property at all, then it is not a property that contributes to a being's perfection. That's contrary to the premises that

- existence is a perfection – premise 2 of the simple reconstruction; and
- I clearly and distinctly perceive that existence belongs to the nature or essence of a supremely perfect being – premise 4 of the elaborate reconstruction, since I can hardly perceive what is not there.

But why think that existence is not a property? The mental image test cannot be enough. After all, the concept of being prime does not change a mental image of a number (there is none), but being prime is a property. Where Kant's argument begins and ends is hard to tell, but he goes on to illustrate:

> A hundred actual dollars do not contain the least bit more than a hundred possible ones. For since the latter signifies the concept and the former its object and its positing in itself, then, in case the former contained more than the latter, my concept would not express the entire object and thus would not be the suitable concept of it. (1998: 567)

If existence were a property, then the concept of a hundred possible (not existing) dollars would be different from the concept of a hundred actual (existing) dollars. And then the concept of a hundred possible dollars would not correspond to the dollars. Similarly, later:

> when I think a thing, through whichever and however many predicates I like (even in its thoroughgoing determination), not the least bit gets added to the thing when I posit in addition that this thing *is*. For otherwise what would exist would not be the same as what I had thought in my concept, but more than that, and I could not say that the very object of my concept exists. (1998: 567–68, bold traded for italics)

If existence were a property, then my concepts would not correspond to the objects in the world in the right way. My concepts would fall short, would be defective. But my concepts do correspond to the objects. For example, my concept of the dollars corresponds to the dollars. Thus existence is not a property.

Why does Kant think that concepts would not correspond to the objects if there is some mismatch between the concept and the object? After all, our concepts often correspond to objects where there is *a lot* of mismatch. For example, people in opposite parties think opposite things about their presidential nominee. Their respective concepts cannot then both match perfectly to the nominee; at least one side gets the nominee *badly* wrong. But their concepts correspond to the nominee. They are thinking about the same person, albeit in different ways.

Kant's thoughts, and the reasoning behind them, are obscure. However, even if Kant's *argument* fails, the *conclusion* that existence is not a property might still be true. And a proper consideration of whether existence is a property returns us to the debate over Meinongianism (see Sections 2.6–7). As Richard Francks frames Kant's conclusion:

> Existence isn't a property which some things have and some things lack: if something doesn't exist, it isn't a thing which lacks existence, it just isn't a thing at all. ... [T]he statement "God exists" isn't a statement about God at all. Rather than being a statement about God, telling us that he exists, it is a statement about the world, about reality, telling us that it contains God. Its logical form is better represented not as "God exists", but as "There is a God", or "Reality includes God". (2008: 157; compare Dicker 2013: 237–42)

The first idea that existence is had by some things but not others is Meinongianism – that there are two realms, a realm of things that exist and a realm of things that do not exist but subsist. The second idea that there are no nonexistent things is just the denial of Meinongianism. The objection thus hinges on the fate of Meinongianism. If Meinongianism is false, then Descartes's argument fails; if it is true, it might still fail, but not for the reason given by Kant (see Miravalle 2018: 80–81).

Kant's objection was for some time taken to be devastating against ontological arguments generally. But Plantinga questions:

> Couldn't Anselm thank Kant for this interesting point and proceed merrily on his way? Where did he try to define God into being by adding existence to a list of properties that defined some concept? According to the great German philosopher and pessimist Arthur Schopenhauer, the ontological argument arises when "someone excogitates a conception, composed out of all sorts of predicates, among which, however, he takes care to include the predicate actuality or existence, either openly or wrapped up for decency's sake in some other predicate, such as perfection, immensity, or something of the kind." If this were Anselm's procedure – if he had simply added existence to a concept that has application contingently if at all – then indeed his argument would be subject to the Kantian criticism. But he didn't, and it isn't. (1974: 97–98)

However, the objection might apply to Anselm after all, insofar as Anselm's argument depends on Meinongianism (see Section 2.5).

3.8 Necessity

A popular way of bypassing Kant's objection is to frame the ontological argument in terms of *necessary existence* instead of mere *existence*. A being would have

- *necessary existence* just in case it could not have failed to exist; or
- *contingent existence* just in case it could have failed to exist.

People, plants, and planets exist contingently, because we could easily have failed to exist: imagine some cosmic catastrophe resulted in our never arriving on the scene. In contrast, God is usually taken to have a stronger grip on reality. God would exist necessarily – if God exists at all.

The reply goes that, whether or not existence is a property, necessary existence is a robust property. Thus Timothy O'Connor:

> Whether Kant is right or not on the propertyhood of existence, however, is beside the point. For what is distinctive of necessary being is not the fact of its existing, but that it enjoys *necessary existence*. And this very much is a substantial, distinctive property, involving a superior mode of existing. The natures of other things (whether instanced or not) will include the property, *being a contingent being* – that is, existing contingently, if at all. And the difference between these two classes of things is evidently intrinsic and fundamental. (2008: 71)

Descartes himself mentions necessary existence, though he might mean by it something a bit different from what we mean (and note how the passage advertises intellectual insight more than argument, *a la* Nolan):

> I ask my readers to spend a great deal of time and effort on contemplating the nature of the supremely perfect being. Above all they should reflect on the fact that the ideas of all other natures contain possible existence, whereas the idea of God contains not only possible but wholly necessary existence. This alone, without a formal argument, will make them realize that God exists; and this will eventually be just as self-evident to them as the fact that the number two is even or that three as odd, and so on. (1984: 115)

The objection that existence is not a property is avoided simply by framing the ontological argument in terms of *necessary existence*: e.g., a perfect being has every perfection; necessary existence is a perfection; therefore, a perfect being has necessary existence; therefore, a perfect being exists.

Focusing on necessary existence might also answer Caterus's objection (see Maydole 2009: 571). The objection would now have to be framed in terms of a *necessarily existing lion*. But Descartes could demur that a *necessary existing lion* is not possible: a lion could only be a contingent thing, given how it depends on its parts, physics, and biology. That might be the crucial difference – if a perfect being could necessarily exist. More on that in Section 4.5.

3.9 Ambiguity

Another objection against Descartes's argument applies most easily against the simple reconstruction. The argument trades on an ambiguity. Sentences of the form "a . . . is . . . " or "a . . . has . . . " can be read in two ways. When these are spelled out carefully in our case, the argument is shown to fail (see van Inwagen 2009: 121–22; Priest 2018: 250–52).

- Reading 1: Sometimes a sentence of that form tells us that there is a certain object. For example, "a cat is on a mat" or "a cat has a mouse" tells us that there is a certain cat. Now premise 1 in the simple reconstruction can be read like this: There is a perfect being with every perfection.

But why accept this premise? An agnostic audience will not accept the premise without further argument. Indeed, the premise now explicitly assumes what the argument is trying to prove: to say that there is a perfect being is to say that a perfect being exists. The argument begs the question.

- Reading 2: Sometimes a sentence of the relevant form tells us only that *if* a certain object exists, *then* it is a certain way. For example, "a unicorn has a horn" does not tell us that there is any unicorn, only that *if* there is a unicorn, *then* it has a horn. Now premise 1 can be read like this: *if* there is a perfect being, then it has every perfection, and the conclusion is that, *if* there is a perfect being, then a perfect being exists.

This conclusion is very plausible, quite independent of the premises. But it is perfectly conditional. The conclusion is no longer that a perfect being exists. Compare Roslyn Weiss's diagnosis of Anselm's argument: Anselm proves that God could only be an existing thing, but not that any existing thing is God (see Weiss 2017; Rowe 1976).

On reading 1, the conclusion is that a perfect being exists, but the premises require further support or quite explicitly assume what they try to prove. On reading 2, the premises as well as the conclusion are plausible, but the conclusion is not that a perfect being exists. Either way, the argument lends scant support to the conclusion that a perfect being exists. The objection remains even if we replace "existence" with "necessary existence."

Dicker (2013: 242–54) reads essentially the same objection into another passage from Caterus:

> Even if it is granted that a supremely perfect being carries the implication of existence in virtue of its very title, it still does not follow that the existence in question is anything actual in the real world; all that follows is that the concept of existence is inseparably linked to the concept of a supreme being. (1986: 98–99)

Caterus grants that a perfect being must exist but objects that the existence of a perfect being does not follow – as per reading 2. But whether and where the ambiguity hides in the elaborate reconstruction of Descartes's argument is not as obvious. The ambiguity might sneak in where the premises say that some property (such as existence) can be "truly affirmed" of something: the premise can be read in two ways, as stating that

- *there is* something of which the property can be truly affirmed; or alternatively that
- *if* there is that thing, then the property can be truly affirmed of it,

where, again, the first reading begs the question and the second has an impotent conclusion.

In any case, the argument might be saved from the objection by Meinongianism or something close enough. Thus Miravalle in the context of this objection answers that

> we may say all kinds of unqualifiedly true things about objects, whether we know them to exist or not. . . . How do we know a triangle has three sides if it exists? Because we know what a triangle is whether it exists or not. How do we know that God is perfect if he exists? Because we know what God is before we know whether he exists. (2018: 79)

Similarly, the premise can state that a perfect being has all perfections without assuming its existence and without any conditional qualification either. The objection has us read the premise as assuming the existence of the being in question or else as some sort of impotent conditional. This overlooks another reading of the premise – simply, that a perfect being has every perfection.

Or, in terms of the distinction between subsistence and existence (see Section 2.9): the audience of the argument begins by admitting the first premise that a perfect being has all perfections, assuming not its existence but its subsistence. However, upon recognizing the second premise, that existence is a perfection, the audience discovers that the perfect being cannot merely subsist – it must exist.

Whether this reply works gets us entangled, once again, in the debate over Meinongianism. And, again, since most of the audience of the ontological argument will not accept Meinongianism, the argument will not be very persuasive.

3.10 Conclusion

The most popular objection against Descartes's ontological argument is that it fails in taking existence to be a property. The objection is problematic: it is hard to show that existence is not a property or that this matters. Nevertheless, the argument remains hostage to other tricky metaphysical questions.

4 Plantinga

4.1 Modality

Let's skip another few centuries from Descartes to Plantinga. Plantinga (1974; 1974a) presents a modal ontological argument. Modal arguments make use of the notions of *possibility* and *necessity* and, often enough, of

• *possible worlds*: ways the world could have gone.

The way things actually are is thus a possible world (the actual world), as is the way in which there is a unicorn (a merely possible world). Next, there is the notion of a

• *necessary being*: a being that could not have failed to exist,

or, in the previously provided terms, that exists in all possible worlds. Plantinga's argument tries to show that there is a necessary being, and that this being is omnipotent, omniscient, and omnibenevolent too. His argument is framed in terms of *maximal excellence* and *maximal greatness*. The excellence of a being in some world depends only on the virtues it instantiates in *that* world. So

• a *maximally excellent being* would be omnipotent, omniscient, and perfectly good in its world.

The greatness of a being depends on its excellence *across* worlds. So

• a *maximally great being* would be maximally excellent in every world.

With these terms in place, the argument proceeds quickly. Plantinga formulates his argument with just three premises:

1. There is a possible world in which maximal greatness is instantiated.
2. Necessarily, a being is maximally great only if it has maximal excellence in every world.
3. Necessarily, a being has maximal excellence in every world only if it has omniscience, omnipotence, and moral perfection in every world (1974: 111; premises renumbered).

And his reasoning:

> if [1] is true, then there is a possible world *W* such that if it had been actual, then there would have existed a being that was omnipotent, omniscient, and morally perfect; this being, furthermore, would have had these qualities in every possible world. So it follows that if *W* had been actual, it would have been *impossible* that there be no such being. That is, if *W* had been actual,
>
> [4] There is no omnipotent, omniscient, and morally perfect being
>
> would have been an impossible proposition. But if a proposition is impossible in at least one possible world, then it is impossible in every possible world; what is impossible does not vary from world to world. Accordingly [4] is impossible in the *actual* world, i.e., impossible *simpliciter*. But if it is impossible that there be no such being, then there actually exists a being that is omnipotent, omniscient, and morally perfect; this being, furthermore, has these qualities essentially and exists in every possible world. (1974: 111–12)

We can set out a more direct argument from the premises:

1. There is some possible world where maximal greatness is instantiated. (Premise)
2. If so, then there is some world where a being has maximal excellence in every world. (Premise)
3. If there is some world where a being has maximal excellence in every world, then the being has maximal excellence in every world. (Premise)
4. If some being has maximal excellence in every world, then it is omniscient, omnipotent, and omnibenevolent in every world. (Premise)
5. Therefore, some being has maximal excellence in every world. (From 1 through 3)
6. Therefore, some being is omniscient, omnipotent, and omnibenevolent in every world. (From 3 and 4)
7. Therefore, some being is omniscient, omnipotent, and omnibenevolent in the actual world. (From 5)

Premises 2 and 4 are true by the definition of *maximal greatness* and *maximal greatness*. Premise 3 assumes that

• what is possibly necessary is necessary,

or what is necessary in some world is necessary in all. Thus, if it is possibly necessary that there is a maximally excellent being, then it is necessary that there is such a being; if in some world a being has maximal excellence in every world, then it has maximal excellence in every world. Plantinga's own formulation is in terms of impossibility rather than necessity: "if a proposition is impossible in at least one possible world, then it is impossible in every possible world." The idea that what is necessary or impossible is so fixed across worlds is not unquestionable (see Chandler 1976; see Pruss & Rasmussen 2018: 14–29 for a defense). But since most will accept the idea, the argument will not be rejected much at this point.

The big question is about premise 1, the *possibility premise*: Is there some possible world in which a being has maximal greatness? Spelling this out in ordinary terms: Could there have been a being that could not have failed to exist and could not have failed to be omnipotent, omniscient, and perfectly good?

Many familiar objections apply here. There is once again the island parody: replace *maximal greatness* and *maximal excellence* throughout with *maximal island greatness* and *maximal island excellence* – where an island is maximally great just in case it is maximally island excellent in all possible worlds, and so on. And then the usual replies apply again. Rinse, wash, and repeat the treatment of the parody above.

4.2 Possibility

The most controversial premise is the possibility premise:

> The only question of interest, it seems to me, is whether its main premise – that maximal greatness is possibly instantiated – is true. I think it is true; hence I think this version of the ontological argument is sound. (Plantinga 1974: 112)

But Plantinga does not have much to say to motivate the premise. Others have tried, and I will consider just a couple of their arguments here (see Section 6.2 for related arguments).

The Śaṃkara Principle. Alexander Pruss supports the possibility premise on the basis of principle distilled from the Hindu philosopher Adi Shankaracharya (a.k.a. Śaṃkara, 788–820):

• what seems, could be.

The idea is that if something *appears* to be the case, then – whether or not it *actually* is the case – at least it *could* be the case. For example, suppose it appears to you that there is a purple elephant in front of you. Likely you've ingested LSD. Likely there is no purple elephant. Still, a purple elephant is possible – it's not like a square circle. The principle gives the right verdict in this and other cases, and that is a reason for believing it (besides other reasons given by Pruss).

Pruss applies the principle to mystical experience where the subjects appear to experience a maximally great being:

> there is reason to believe, or at least a presumption, that some of the high mystics had an experience *as of* a maximally great being. . . . If Śaṃkara's

principle were true, it would follow that it is possible there is a maximally great being. (Pruss 2001: 112)

Some argue from mystical experience to the existence of God: we should believe that things are as they appear to be, at least in the absence of opposite evidence; and God appears in mystical experiences, or so it seems to those having the experience (see Kwan 2009; Swinburne 2004: chapter 13; compare Gellman 1997). This is not Pruss's strategy. Here he is not taking mystical experiences to directly show that God exists. By the Śaṃkara Principle, he takes mystical experiences to show only that God possibly exists. Then the ontological argument takes us from the possibility to the actual existence of God.

Strictly speaking, the Śaṃkara Principle threatens the ontological argument *as such*. The Principle is

- applied to particular experiences, i.e. mystical experiences; and
- might itself be supported on the basis of experience, as an empirical generalization.

This would mean that the argument relying on it is no longer a perfectly armchair argument. But that's no reason for discounting the argument. If only the big problem was that the argument is not an ontological proof!

Objections. A more serious problem is in counterexamples to the Śaṃkara Principle: experiences where something *appears* to be the case but could *not* possibly be. Pruss describes a dream where he had a "proof" of a mathematical proposition. By the Śaṃkara Principle, the dream experience shows that proof of the proposition is possible. And, if proof is possible, then the proposition is possibly true. But, as it turns out and as Pruss was aware upon awakening, the proof was nonsense and the proposition was not possibly true. Thus the Śaṃkara Principle fails.

To answer this problem, Pruss tells us that the principle should be applied only to how things "*really* seem" (Pruss 2001: 2016): the experience only shows possible what is vivid or transparent enough in experience. For example, suppose he dreamed of receiving a Field Medal for some "proof." He ascends a stage. Someone hands over the medal. Everyone cheers. We can properly apply the principle to these vivid parts of the dream. By the Śaṃkara Principle, Pruss's winning the Field Medal is possible – and surely it is. But the "proof" itself was not a vivid part of the dream. Not a single line of proof appeared in the dream. And so we cannot properly apply the Principle to that part of the dream.

Now the question is whether mystical experiences are more like the experience of winning the Field Medal or the experience of the mathematical "proof." Pruss assures us that many mystical experiences are vivid enough:

> [T]here is, arguably, an agreement between mystics of various religions that they have had an experience of a maximally great reality, a reality than which a greater cannot be conceived. Perhaps on this point one might even adduce not only Western but also Eastern mystics. If there is a widespread agreement among mystics of different theological persuasions about the apparent object of high mystical experiences having maximal greatness, we have reason to think that this agreement is grounded in the phenomenology of the experiences themselves, i.e., that these mystics are indeed having experiences *as of* a maximally great being. (Pruss 2001: 117)

Doubtless, many mystics have vivid experiences that seem to them to be of God. But whether they have experiences that seem to be of a *maximally great being* is more doubtful. Nagasawa objects that

> it seems far from obvious that there would be any phenomenal differences that humans could detect between, for example, experiences *as of* God, as a maximally excellent being existing in all possible worlds, and experiences *as of* a maximally excellent being existing in all but one remote possible world. (2017: 1991)

Nagasawa questions whether the mystical experiences appear to their subjects to be of

- maximal excellence: omnipotence, omniscience, and omnibenevolence; or
- maximal greatness: omnipotence, omniscience, omnibenevolence plus *necessary existence,*

and doubts that maximal greatness can be distinguished enough from maximal excellence in the mystical experiences. If maximal greatness is not experienced vividly enough, then mystical experiences do not show the possibility of maximal greatness via the Śaṃkara Principle. They might show the possibility of maximal excellence, though Nagasawa also questions whether omnipotence can be distinguished enough from near-omnipotence in mystical experience. In any case, the possibility of maximal excellence is not enough for the possibility premise of the ontological argument (see Byerly 2010 for further objections).

The Value Argument. Joshua Rasmussen – who is luminous – presents an argument for the possibility premise as follows:

1. Some degree of value can be instantiated.
2. If some degree of value can be instantiated, then each degree of value can be instantiated.
3. Therefore, each degree of value can be instantiated. (From 1 and 2)
4. Maximal greatness is a degree of value.

5. Therefore, maximal greatness can be instantiated. (From 3 and 4) (2018: 183; premise numbering and indicators changed)

This resembles an argument in Anselm's reply to Gaunilo:

> since every lesser good, insofar as it is good, is similar to a greater good, it is clear to every reasonable mind that by raising our thoughts from lesser goods to greater goods, we can certainly form an idea of that than which a greater cannot be thought on the basis of those things than which a greater can be thought. (1995: 44)

Whereas Anselm argues from the idea of a lesser value to the idea of maximum value, Rasmussen argues from the possibility of lesser value to the possibility of maximum value (see Burns 2018 for treatment of a similar argument from Iris Murdoch). Rasmussen summarizes:

> One starts by seeing that there is value in the world. One then recognizes that mere differences in degree of value don't apparently make a difference with respect to possible instantiation. One thereby gains a reason to infer that each degree of value can be instantiated. Maximal greatness is a degree of value. Therefore, one has reason to infer that maximal greatness can be instantiated. Therefore, one has reason to think there can be a maximally great being. (2018: 184)

Premise 1 is plausible: if some degree of value is had, then some degree *can* be had; and some degree is had. For example, this book has some value – hopefully as a book, but at least as a fan.

Premise 2 is trickier. Rasmussen supports the premise via a general principle of

- modal continuity: where properties differ only in degrees, then either all are possible or all are impossible.

For example, the properties of being one mile, being two miles, being three miles, and so forth, differ in degrees and all are equally possible. There are some exceptions (e.g., being a three-sided triangle is possible; being a two-sided triangle is not), but in such cases, there is a relevant difference between the objects. The presumption is that value is no exception: "If some particular degree of value is possible, then why is any other not possible? What difference could there be between one degree of value and another that could explain why the one is possible but the other is impossible?" (Rasmussen 2018: 184).

Finally, premise 3 follows from maximal greatness being a specific value, or quantity of value, or point along the continuum – any point counts, even the special point at the far end.

Objections. Rasmussen considers an objection from a *failure* of value argument that mirrors the value argument: since some degree of value can *fail* to be had, each degree of value can similarly fail to be had, and thus maximal greatness can fail to be had. If maximal greatness is possible, then it cannot fail to be had – maximal greatness would have to be had in every possible world. Thus maximal greatness is not possible. The failure of value argument points in the opposite direction to the value argument but is equally plausible. We have a stalemate, without any reason to favor the value argument and the possibility premise.

In reply, Rasmussen challenges the initial assumption of the failure of value argument: that some degree of value can fail to be had. Whereas we do discover some degree of value, we do not discover the absence of any degree of value. We might discover the absence of a degree of value here or there, or now or then. But that is not to discover the complete absence of that degree of value anywhere; value might be had *somewhere* far away from us.

However, here is another presumptive principle of continuity:

- if something can be absent from some place and time, then it can be absent from all places and times.

For example, if a cat can be absent from *here*, then why could it not be absent from *there*? And if it could be absent from there, why could it not be absent from everywhere? What difference could there be between times and places that could explain why the cat could be absent from some but not from others? There might similarly be a presumption that a degree of value absent somewhere can be absent everywhere. Then the failure of value argument is salvaged from Rasmussen's reply.

Rasmussen floats a proposal:

> [O]ne could theorize that the greatest conceivable value entails every degree of value. This proposal is an instance of the general theory that greater degrees include lower degrees, where the lower degrees are positive, modally continuous degrees. A ten-dollar bill, for example, includes the value of nine dollars: after all, you could use a ten-dollar bill to buy something that costs nine dollars. ... The result is that if there were a greatest conceivable being, then all values would be instantiated, regardless of the lack of values you and I may experience. (2018: 186)

Showing that maximal greatness is had might show that every degree of value is had even while some degree of value is not had here and now, and thus rebut the presumption that a degree of value absent somewhere can be absent everywhere. But we have not yet shown that maximal greatness *is* had.

Finally, premise 4 looks very close to the conclusion: What is it for maximal greatness to be a degree of value if it cannot possibly be instantiated? The question of whether there is a maximum of greatness has already been raised (see Section 2.9), but the following sections treat objections that are supposed to show the traditional attributes making up this greatness impossible.

4.3 Paradoxes

If omnipotence, omniscience, and omnibenevolence are not possible, then a maximally excellent being, and thus a maximally great being, is not possible, contrary to premise 1. Some argue that some of the properties are not possible. For example, the paradox of the stone is supposed to show that omnipotence is impossible: Can an omnipotent being create a stone it cannot lift? If it can create the stone, then it is not omnipotent because then there could be something it cannot lift; and if it cannot create the stone, then it is not omnipotent because there is something it cannot create (see Mavrodes 1973). Or so the argument goes.

Others argue that while each of the properties might be possible, their combination is impossible. For example, the paradox of omnipotence and omnibenevolence is supposed to show that the combination of these properties is impossible: Can an omnipotent being do something wrong? If it can, then it is not omnibenevolent; if it cannot, then it is not omnipotent (see Morriston 2001). Or so the argument goes.

4.4 Ambition

Theists usually answer such paradoxes on a case-by-case basis (see Hoffman & Rosenkrantz 2002; Swinburne 2016). For example, some answer the paradox of the stone by pointing out that while there *could* be something an omnipotent being cannot do, there is nothing it cannot do *unless and until* it does create the stone. Working through all the paradoxes and answers can be tedious. Fortunately, Nagasawa has proposed a simple answer promising to eliminate the threat posed by all the paradoxes:

> My new response to the arguments against perfect being theism is to replace the omni God thesis [that God must be omnipotent, omniscient and omnibenevolent] with the following thesis:
> > The Maximal God thesis: God is the being that has the maximal consistent set of knowledge, power, and benevolence.
> The maximal God thesis suggests that, while God is certainly very knowledgeable, very powerful, and very benevolent, He might or might not be omniscient, omnipotent, and omnibenevolent. (2017: 92)

Keep the ontological argument as is, but spell out *maximal excellence* in terms of a being than which no greater is metaphysically possible: a maximally excellent being is overall greater than any other possible being. This might mean that a maximally excellent being is omnipotent, omniscient, and omnibenevolent. But, if the paradoxes work and these turn out to be impossible, the maximally excellent being can still have as impressive a combination of power, knowledge, and goodness as is possible. Thus, even if there could not be an omnipotent, omniscient, or omnibenevolent being, the ontological argument proves that there is as impressive a being as there *could* be.

Nagasawa's strategy is designed to avoid the paradoxes and to secure premise 1 of the ontological argument. The strategy shows how a little redefinition can save the possibility of maximal excellence from the paradoxes. As Nagasawa summarizes:

> [W]e can automatically derive that it is possible that God exists because here God is understood as the being that has the *maximal* consistent set of knowledge, power, and benevolence. In other words, the maximal concept of God is *by definition* internally coherent because its components are mutually consistent (and internally coherent). This guarantees the possibility of the existence of God. (2017: 204)

He concludes that "the possibility premise, arguably the only controversial premise of the modal ontological argument, is established and the argument successfully derives the existence of God" (2017: 205).

4.5 Compossibility

Here is one worry: there is no final point before a meter mark; 0.9 m is followed by 0.99 m, 0.99 m by 0.999 m, and so on. Similarly, perhaps, there might be no maximal consistent set of properties less than omniscience, omnipotence, and omnibenevolence. Here's another worry we can focus on: even if Nagasawa shows the set possible, he does not show the properties possible together with necessary existence. Premise 1 requires not only the possibility of maximal excellence but the possibility of maximal excellence together with necessary existence – maximal greatness.

Whether maximal excellence can be combined with necessary existence is not transparent. The possibility of an impressive enough combination of knowledge, power, and goodness is secured because these properties come in degrees – an impressive enough degree of one is possible together with another. But necessary existence does not come in degrees.

Is the possibility of combining necessary existence with maximal excellence any easier than the possibility of combining necessary existence with, say, the property of being a particle? The proponent of the ontological argument wants the conclusion that a maximally excellent being must exist, but not the conclusion that some particle must exist; at least traditional theists usually take physical objects to be created and not sharing necessary existence. The problem now is to show that necessary existence can be combined with maximal excellence but not with being a particle.

4.6 Polytheism

Problems multiply–as does the number of divine beings the ontological argument points toward, since necessary existence might just as easily be compatible with various combinations of quite divine attributes. There might be a number of possible maximally excellent beings: for example, if omnipotence is at odds with omnibenevolence, then one possibility is a being with more power and another is a being with more goodness, where both beings might be equally impressive overall. Following Nagasawa, suppose that 10 units is the maximum measure for each of omnipotence, omniscience, and omnibenevolence. Suppose that a combined maximum of 30 is impossible for any being because of some paradox about the attributes. Could we not have two maximally excellent natures each, with 29 units in total,

- one with 10 units of power, 9 units of knowledge, and 10 units of goodness; and
- another with 9 units of power, 10 units of knowledge, and 10 units of goodness?

Or consider the possibilities of an essentially temporally eternal divine being versus an essentially atemporal divine being. If each nature can be combined with necessary existence, then there will be two or more necessary divine beings.
    Nagasawa answers that

> even if we accept the possibility that God does not possess omniscience, omnipotence, and omnibenevolence, we do not have to commit ourselves to the possibility that another being reaches the same axiological value as God by having a different combination of knowledge, power, and benevolence (2017: 112).

For example,

- maximum knowledge might be 9 units – so that the second being could have at most 28 units, and thus less than the maximally excellent nature of 29 units; or
- power, knowledge, and goodness might not be equally weighted – so that the second being is not maximally excellent, even with 29 units.

The assumption that the two natures would be equally impressive is disputable, but so is the opposite assumption. In any case, there could be two *quite* divine natures, even if unequal. Elsewhere Nagasawa says that we should not worry about a second-greatest nature. The possibility

> does not mean that the second greatest possible being is *actual*. Given that such a being does not reach the maximal greatness of God as the being than which no greater is metaphysically possible, perfect being theists do not need to think that the ontological argument entails the existence of such a being. And since there is no evidence for the existence of such a being, we can assume that it is a merely possible being. (2017: 110)

But the problem now is to show that necessary existence can be combined with one quite divine nature but not another. Otherwise, the ontological argument points no more to one divine being than to countless other quite divine beings. Since Nagasawa has not shown this, his project is incomplete (compare Arbour n.d.; Leftow 1988).

4.7 Impossibility

Richard Gale objects that premise 1 conflicts with more plausible modal intuitions. He looks for a property that:

> (i) intuitively seems more likely to admit of the possibility of instantiation than does having unsurpassable greatness and (ii) is *strongly incompatible* with it in that if either property is instantiated in any possible world, the other is instantiated in none. (1991: 195; compare Rowe 1987: 71–72)

Gale focuses on the possibility of unjustified evils – evils a maximally excellent being would never allow. His example is of a supernova annihilating a planet of happy and good creatures. If a maximally great being is possible, then every possible world contains a maximally excellent being. A maximally excellent being would prevent the supernova since it has power and reason enough to prevent it, and so no possible world would contain the supernova. But the supernova is possible. Therefore, a maximally great being is not possible.
   More generally:

> There is no possible world in which both God, an unsurpassingly great being, and morally unjustified evil exist, since it is a conceptual truth that God is both willing and able to prevent such an evil. But if the property of having unsurpassable greatness is instantiated in any world, it is instantiated in every one. Therefore, the possibility [of maximal greatness] is logically incompatible with [the possibility of a morally unjustified evil]. (1991: 196)

The usual problem of evil is about apparently unjustified evil: Why would God permit such evil? The usual religious response is that, contrary to appearances, the evil could be justified. But the problem now is not the appearance of unjustified evil, but the appearance of the *possibility* of unjustified evil (see Conee 2005: 92–93). Even if there actually is no unjustified evil, is it not so much as possible?

Gale also draws on the possibility of everyone always freely choosing to do evil at any moral decision: if a maximally great being is possible, then every possible world contains a maximally excellent being; no maximally excellent being would bring about people who always freely choose evil, and so no world would contain such people; therefore, a maximally great being is not possible.

The argument assumes that a maximally excellent being would have "middle knowledge" – would know what the people would freely do without their actually doing it, and so would not bring them about. Since Plantinga accepts the doctrine of middle knowledge, the argument might be good ad hominem. But the doctrine is so controversial that the argument will be less useful than the argument from the possibility of unjustified evils.

4.8 Intuitions

Oppy criticizes the arguments from the possibility of unjustified evil and the possibility of everyone always freely choosing evil:

> Gale's argument is subject to a dilemma: Either these alleged possibilities are compatible with the existence of God or they are not. If they are, then a theist can accept them; but if they are not, then a theist will reject them. (1995: 255)

The possibility of unjustified evil can be rejected in favor of the possibility of maximal greatness. The theist should accept that God is "the delimiter of possibilities" (Morris 1987: 48). But Gale's objection might still have an audience. Gale's point is not to convert theists. The point of the ontological argument – one of its points – is to convert agnostics or atheists. And so long as the unjustified evil is more plausibly possible than is maximal greatness, *they* should jettison maximal greatness instead.

Oppy further argues:

> Moreover, a theist who rejects these possibilities need not be obviously irrational: For, if I hold that God exists and that the existence of God is incompatible with the existence of morally unjustified evil, then of course I will hold that it is not possible that there is morally unjustified evil. But why should it not turn out that I have a very strong intuition that it is possible that unsurpassable greatness is instantiated? (1995: 255–56)

There *need not* be anything irrational in holding onto the possibility of maximal greatness. But Gale's objection still has force: so long as unjustified evil is more plausibly possible than is maximal greatness, maximal greatness should be jettisoned instead. Someone with a stronger intuition that unjustified evil is possible would be irrational in holding, without further argument, onto the intuition that maximal greatness is possible.

4.9 Question-Begging

Ontological arguments are often accused of begging the question. An argument usually begs the question if acceptance of the premises depends on prior acceptance of the conclusion. Then the argument should not persuade. Plantinga provides this example of a useless proof:

> Either God exists or $7 + 5 = 14$
> It is false that $7 + 5 = 14$
> Therefore God exists (1974: 112)

Even if the premises are all true and the logic is valid, the argument fails because "no one who didn't already accept the conclusion, would accept the first premise" (1974: 112). Acceptance of the premise could only depend upon prior acceptance of the conclusion. Contrast the ontological argument:

> The ontological argument we've been examining isn't just like this one, of course, but it must be conceded that not everyone who understands and reflects on its central premise – that the existence of a maximally great being is *possible* – will accept it. Still, it is evidence, I think, that there is nothing *contrary to reason* or *irrational* in accepting the premise. What I claim for this argument, therefore, is that it establishes, not the *truth* of theism, but its rational acceptability. (1974: 112)

Plantinga insists that accepting premise 1 is rational. This is nothing like self-evident. He takes the premise to be just like so many other respectable philosophical principles – and they had better be respectable and rational or else we would be left with "a pretty slim and pretty dull philosophy" (Plantinga 1974a: 221). This will not inspire philosophical pessimists. But if it does inspire, then the point can apply *directly* to the conclusion too: theism is about as rational and respectable as any controversial philosophical view. Then, even if there is nothing irrational in accepting the possibility premise, the premise, along with the rest of the ontological argument, is otiose (see van Inwagen 2018: 246–47).

However, even if there is nothing irrational in accepting the possibility premise, that does not save the argument from begging the question. If there were nothing irrational in believing in a maximally great being, there would be nothing irrational in subsequently accepting the possibility premise; after all, there being a maximal great being entails that a maximally great being is possible, and that maximal greatness is possibly instantiated. However, the grounds for accepting premise 1 would be prior acceptance of the conclusion, and the argument would remain question-begging.

Does acceptance of the possibility premise not depend upon acceptance of the conclusion? Ontological arguments are sometimes described as arguments from the possibility of God to his actuality. Some atheists accept that, while not actual, God is at least metaphysically possible. So it might be thought that they accept the possibility premise, without accepting the conclusion – and thus that ontological arguments should convince them by connecting the premise to the conclusion.

However, when atheists accept the possibility of God, they might accept only the possibility of maximal excellence, not maximal greatness. If so, they accept less than the possibility premise. For Plantinga's ontological argument to bite, enough of an audience would need to accept the premise prior to accepting the conclusion. Rowe asks:

> What then do we have to know in order to know that God (a maximally great being) is a *possible* being? At a minimum ... we have to *know* that an omniscient, omnipotent, morally perfect being exists in the *actual world*. For, putting aside other possible worlds, if such a being doesn't exist in the possible world that is actual, he isn't what Plantinga defines him to be: a maximally great being. Indeed, if he doesn't exist in the possible world that is *actual*, he is an *impossible* being. (2009: 89)

The possibility of maximal greatness very quickly entails (by definition) the possibility of necessary existence, which quite quickly entails existence. While the premise that maximal greatness is possible does not say – explicitly – that God exists, it so *nearly* does. We have seen some attempts to support the possibility premise independently of the conclusion and found these wanting (see Sections 4.2–5 and Sections 6.1–2 for other attempts). In the absence of such support, the premise and the conclusion are so close that acceptance of the premise will depend on a prior acceptance of the conclusion, and the argument begs the question. Van Inwagen takes question-begging to be the big problem with *all* modal ontological arguments (e.g., Hartshorne 1962: chapter 2):

> The modal ontological argument – in any of its versions, for they all have a "possibility" premise, a premise of the same sort as "It is possible for there to be a necessary existent being that has all perfections essentially" – suffers from only one defect: there seems to be no *a priori* reason, or none accessible to the human intellect ... to think that it is possible for there to be a necessary existent being that has all perfections essentially. I myself think this premise is true – but only because I think there in fact *is* a necessary existent being who has all perfections essentially. And my reason for thinking that are by no means *a priori*. (van Inwagen 2018: 243)

By the way, here is an apparently question-begging argument:

1. Some valid arguments have only particular premises.
2. Therefore, some valid arguments have only particular premises. (Sinnott-Armstrong 1999: 176, renumbered; also see Sorensen 1991)

where a *particular premise* is just a premise of the form of the first premise. Should this argument not convince us of the conclusion?

4.10 Conclusion

Plantinga's ontological argument is elegant. But the central premise is tricky. We have questioned some attempts to support it. I think that the premises are true and the logic tight, and thus that the argument is sound. But I accept the possibility premise only because I *already* accept the conclusion. I do not think the argument should persuade a wide audience.

5 Lowe

5.1 Modesty

Jonathan Lowe (2013) defends ontological arguments of the kind presented thus far. But he also defends a quite different argument. The argument also focuses on necessary existence and the premises are supposed to be knowable *a priori*. So it is advertised as a modal ontological argument. Fortunately, unlike other modal arguments, his does not depend on a controversial possibility premise (2012: 187–88). Unfortunately, the conclusion focused on is just that a concrete being necessarily exists, where

- *concrete* beings exist in space or time; as opposed to
- *abstract* beings that are spaceless and timeless.

Though Lowe hints that the being must also be a powerful mind, the argument does not promise to show omnipotence, omniscience, and omnibenevolence. In this way, it is less ambitious than the other ontological arguments covered.

   On the definitions given, the argument would show that there is a necessary being in space or time. Some take God to exist in time, and thus in space *or* time. But God is often taken to exist outside space and time. To preserve divine timelessness, the argument could be run on alternative definitions of

- *concrete* beings as beings with causal powers, whether spatiotemporal or not, as opposed to
- *abstract* beings that are impotent.

Lowe's premises and conclusions can be brought together as follows:

1. Some necessary abstract beings exist. (Premise)
2. All abstract beings are dependent beings. (Premise)
3. All dependent beings depend for their existence on independent beings. (Premise)
4. Therefore, all abstract beings depend for their existence on concrete beings. (From 2 and 3)
5. The existence of any dependent being needs to be explained. (Premise)
6. Therefore, the existence of necessary abstract beings needs to be explained. (From 1, 2, and 5)
7. Dependent beings of any kind cannot explain their own existence. (Premise)
8. The existence of dependent beings can only be explained by beings on which they depend for their existence. (Premise)
9. Therefore, the existence of necessary abstract beings can only be explained by concrete beings. (From 4, 2, 7, and 8)
10. No contingent being can explain the existence of a necessary being. (Premise)
11. Therefore, the existence of necessary abstract beings is explained by one or more necessary concrete beings. (From 6, 9, and 10)
12. Therefore, a necessary concrete being exists. (From 11) (Lowe 2012: 184–87; renumbered and reorganized with premise indicators)

So far as the argument stands, the necessary concrete being might be an atom or a lion. However, Lowe takes the argument to point toward a powerful mind. Jettisoning the numbered premises and conclusions at this point, Lowe addresses the question of whether all abstract beings are dependent:

> A clue here, however, is provided by the very expression "abstract". An abstract being, it would seem, is one which, by its very nature, is in some sense *abstracted* – literally, "drawn out of, or away from" – *something else*. To that extent, then, any such being may reasonably be supposed to *depend for its existence* on that *from* which it is "abstracted". All of the most plausible examples of abstract beings are, interestingly enough, entities which are, in a broad sense, *objects of reason* – such entities as *numbers*, *sets*, and *propositions*. They are all objects which stand in *rational* relations to one another, such as mathematical and logical relations. Very arguably, however, it does not make sense to think of such entities as existing and standing in such relations independently of some actual or possible mind which could contemplate and understand them. But then we have a very good candidate for the sort of being "from" which such entities may be supposed to be somehow "abstracted": namely, a *mind* of some kind, upon which they would thereby *depend for their existence*. (2012: 189)

In light of the above, we could update the previous argument with the following premise:

13. If the existence of necessary abstract beings is explained by one or more necessary concrete beings, then the necessary abstract beings are explained by one or more necessarily existing rational minds. (Premise)
14. Therefore, a rational mind necessarily exists. (From 11 and 13)

While Lowe's ontological argument does not closely resemble Plantinga's, the point here does closely resemble another argument from Plantinga:

> *The Argument from (Natural) Numbers.* (I once heard Tony Kenny attribute a particularly elegant version of this argument to Bob Adams.) It also seems plausible to think of numbers as dependent upon or even constituted by intellectual activity; indeed, students always seem to think of them as "ideas" or "concepts," as dependent, somehow, upon our intellectual activity. So if there were no minds, there would be no numbers. . . . But again, there are too many of them for them to arise as a result of human intellectual activity. We should therefore think of them as among God's ideas. (Plantinga 2007: 213)

The treatment of Lowe's ontological argument will bring us toward one of a family of arguments related to ontological arguments, insofar as they rely on pretty abstract or *a priori* metaphysical principles (see Pruss & Rasmussen 2018: chapter 7, for an especially similar argument).

5.2 Truthmakers

While Lowe's argument does without a controversial possibility premise, it has many premises of its own – and every new premise is a new pressure point. But Lowe motivates the most controversial premises. We'll work through a few of them briefly, especially premises 1, 2, 3, and 10.

As for premise 1, the necessary abstract beings Lowe has in mind are the numbers:

> necessary abstract beings include *numbers* – for instance, the natural numbers, 0, 1, 2, 3, and so on *ad infinitum*. Why should we suppose that these numbers exist? Simply because there are mathematical truths concerning them – such as the truth that $2 + 3 = 5$ – and these truths are *necessary* truths, i.e., true *in every possible world*. The natural numbers are the *truthmakers* of such truths – the entities in virtue of whose existence those truths obtain – and hence those numbers must exist *in every possible world*, in order to make those truths obtain in every possible world. (Lowe 2012: 181)

Truths generally are made true by things in the world. For example, the sentence "the cat is on the mat" is true because of the cat, the mat, and their spatial positions. Similarly, the truths of arithmetic are made true – they are true because of the numbers and their connections to each other. Numbers are the essential ingredients of arithmetical truths. But since arithmetical truths are necessarily true, their essential ingredients must necessarily exist. Thus numbers necessarily exist. Also, numbers are not concrete – you could never bump into the number 2 or 3. They're essentially abstract. Therefore, in the necessary existence of numbers, we have the necessary existence of some abstract beings.

5.3 Dependence

Premise 2 rules out the possibility of independent abstract beings. Lowe takes abstract beings to depend on other beings in this sense: "*F*s depend for their existence on *G*s df= necessarily, *F*s exist only if *G*s exist" (2012: 182). The premise is illustrated in the case of sets: sets are abstract beings and are dependent, since they depend on their members. The empty set would be a counterexample – a set that does not have, and thus does not depend on, any member. But Lowe does not countenance the possibility of an empty set:

> I think we ought to be sceptical about the very existence of the so-called empty set: I believe that it is a mere mathematical fiction. . . . After all, how could there really be any such thing as *a set* with *no* members, when what a set *is*, according to our common understanding, is something that "collects together" certain other things, these things being its members. How could *something* "collect together" nothing? (2012: 183)

Compare Michael Huemer: "Do we really understand the idea that there is a collection when there is nothing at all that is collected?" (2016: 108). If there could be no empty set, then all sets must depend on their members.

5.4 Grounding

Premise 3 rules out the possibility of abstract beings depending only on other abstract beings. If all abstract beings depend only on other abstract beings, then we would end up with either

- a weird circle of dependence, with being *a* depending on being *b*, and being *b* depending on being *c*, and being *c* . . . depending on being *a*.
- an infinite chain of dependence, with being *a* depending on being *b*, and being *b* depending on being *c*, and being *c* depending on being *d* . . . all the way down forever.

Lowe rejects the unacceptable "consequence that the existence of some or all abstract entities is not properly *grounded*" (2012: 182). Abstract beings must then depend on independent beings. But, as per premise 2, *all* abstract beings are dependent. Premise 4 follows: abstract beings must depend on concrete beings.

At this point, Lowe's argument becomes complicated by bringing together principles about dependence and explanation. Unfortunately, Lowe does not tell us what exactly he means by *explanation*, and does not provide any reason for accepting the subsequent premises 5, 7, and 10, though they do sound plausible enough. In any case, the argument can be framed in terms of dependence alone without losing too much. In short, since the necessary abstract beings must depend on concrete beings, they must depend on either

- contingent concrete beings, or
- necessary concrete beings.

But necessary beings cannot depend on contingent beings. So the necessary abstract beings must depend on necessary concrete beings. Therefore, a necessary concrete being must exist (contrast Lowe 1998: chapter 12; Coggins 2010: 95–113). The crucial idea here is that necessary beings cannot depend on contingent beings – and this parallels premise 10 about explanation.

5.5 Explanation

Premise 10 rules out explaining necessary abstract beings in terms of contingent concrete beings. If a contingent concrete being explains a necessary abstract being, then had that contingent being not existed, the necessary being would either

- explain itself, or
- have had no explanation at all, or
- be explained by another contingent being.

The first route is ruled out by premises 2 and 7: all abstract beings are dependent, and dependent beings do not explain their own existence. The second route is ruled out by premises 2 and 5: all abstract beings are dependent, and all dependent beings need explanations. The third route is ruled out since what the contingent being

> would purportedly be explaining the existence of is something that exists in every possible world and hence something whose existence far transcends its own. Furthermore, to contend that the existence of a necessary being, N, is explained in different possible worlds by different contingent beings in those worlds threatens to undermine the very *necessity* of N's existence. For then it appears to be a mere cosmic accident that every possible world happens to contain something that is, allegedly, able to explain the existence of N in that world. (2012: 185)

If the existence of a necessary being is explained by the existence of a contingent being, then had the contingent being failed to exist (quite possible for contingent beings) the necessary being would still have to exist (quite necessary for necessary beings) – and so, in place of the original contingent being, another contingent being would have explained the existence of the necessary being. But what good fortune for an alternative contingent being to always be available! Since this is too much of a cosmic coincidence, the existence of a necessary being cannot be explained by the existence of a contingent being.

The same kind of problem arises if we focus just on dependence, without getting entangled in the premises about explanation. If a necessary being could depend on a contingent being, then there would always have to be some contingent being or other for the necessary being to depend on. Since this is too much of a cosmic coincidence, a necessary being could not depend on a contingent being. And what could be preventing the nonexistence of all contingent beings? The necessary being? If so, then the necessary being seems to depend on the contingent beings, even while the contingent beings depend on the necessary being – a weird circle of dependence.

So contingent concrete beings cannot do the metaphysical work. Premise 11 follows: it must be done by necessary concrete beings. And from that in turn the big conclusion follows: a necessary concrete being exists. Add the idea about the abstract beings depending on minds to arrive at an even bigger conclusion: a necessary concrete and powerful mind exists.

5.6 Fictionalism

We turn to objections and replies, especially about the premises we have focused on above. Starting at the top, recall: the first premise is that some necessary abstract beings exist. Lowe takes numbers to be the essential ingredients of the necessary truths of arithmetic, and so concludes that they necessarily exist. But there are rival views about the ingredients and nature of arithmetic. The most radically opposite view is likely

- fictionalism: arithmetic is fiction, sentences like *2 + 3 = 5* are not true, and numbers do not exist.

On the one hand, fictionalism is motivated by parsimony: we avoid all the philosophical puzzles about spooky abstract beings by denying their existence. On the other hand, the view that *2 + 3 = 5* is not true sounds bonkers. In reply, fictionalists distinguish between

- truth simpliciter: for example, *J. K. Rowling is the author of Harry Potter* is true simpliciter but is not true in the fiction of Harry Potter – since J. K. Rowling is not a character in Harry Potter at all; and
- truth in the fiction: for example, *Harry Potter is a wizard* is true in the fiction of *Harry Potter*, but is not true simpliciter – since Harry Potter does not exist at all.

The fictionalist reassures us, then, that *2 + 3 = 5* is true in a sense: it is true in the fiction of arithmetic. Only, it is not true *simpliciter*, outside the fiction, and so requires no truthmakers – numbers need not exist.

Fictionalism is as popular as it is controversial. The fictionalist needs to make sense of why arithmetic is so indispensable in understanding the world – more even than is *Harry Potter*. But there are attempts to answer these and other problems with fictionalism (see Field 1980; Leng 2010), and there are yet other views about the ingredients and nature of arithmetic at odds with the premise (see Craig 2016). A study of these is beyond the scope of this book. Lowe recognizes:

> That necessary *abstract* beings exist, such as numbers, is certainly not entirely uncontroversial, but it is far less controversial than that a necessary *concrete* being exists. Indeed, I would urge that all of the premises of the new argument are individually considerably less controversial than its conclusion. ... And this, really, is the most that one can generally hope to achieve in a philosophical argument: that its premises non-trivially entail its conclusion and that every one of those premises has considerable plausibility and is considerably less controversial than its conclusion. For an argument with these features has the merit of providing us with a persuasive reason to endorse an interesting conclusion which, considered merely on its own, might appear to be implausible. (2012: 188)

No argument for a substantive conclusion in philosophy has uncontroversial premises; the best we get are premises that appeal to enough of an audience. The first premise does well enough at that. But the audience might dwindle further at the second.

5.7 Foundations

Recall: the second premise is that all abstract beings are dependent. Lowe illustrates this for sets. But other abstract beings might not be dependent: maybe propositions, properties, and possibilities are not dependent. Maybe the necessary abstract beings of premise 1 – numbers – could be independent.

Lowe argues elsewhere in more detail that all abstract beings are dependent (see Lowe 1998: chapter 10). He first argues on grounds of parsimony that all abstract beings are either sets or properties. He next argues that sets and properties are dependent. We have already seen how he takes sets to be dependent. Lowe also takes properties to be dependent in this sense: for every property, there must be something that has the property; there could not be a property that floats free. Redness could not exist without red things (e.g., tomatoes) existing. Roundness could not exist without round things (e.g., tomatoes) existing. If sets and properties are the only abstract beings, and sets and properties are dependent, then all abstract beings are dependent.

Lowe argues that just as

- Foundation Principle 1: sets ultimately depend on things that are not sets (their members), so too
- Foundation Principle 2: properties ultimately depend on things that are not properties (particulars).

Just as there can be sets of sets of sets . . . but these must ultimately bottom off in things that are not sets, so too there can be properties had by properties had by properties . . . but these ultimately bottom off in things that are not properties. In his earlier work, Lowe proceeded toward the dependence of abstract beings on concrete beings as follows. Imagine that there could have been only abstract beings – only sets and properties (he calls properties *universals*):

> [T]he only universals which could in principle exist in a world devoid of concrete particulars would be universals whose instances were abstract particulars. And we have assumed that the only abstract particulars are *sets*. Sets, however, can only exist in worlds in which *their members* exist. . . . [I]f only "impure" sets exist, then *non*-sets must exist in addition to sets. Of course, *universals* are non-sets, but there is an obvious difficulty in supposing that there might be a world in which the only non-sets are universals *whose only particular instances are sets*. For in such a world the sets depend for their existence upon the universals and the universals depend for their existence upon the sets, creating a vicious circle. . . . I conclude that there cannot be a world which *only* contains universals and sets and hence cannot be a world in which only abstract objects exist. (Lowe 1998: 253–54)

If there were only abstract beings, the properties would ultimately be had by the sets, since the only abstract beings that are not properties are sets. And the sets would ultimately have properties as their members, since the only abstract beings that are not sets are properties. So the properties would depend on the sets, even while the sets would depend on the properties – an impossible circle of dependence. Therefore, what we originally imagined is not possible after all: there could not be only abstract beings. There must also be concrete beings for the abstract beings to depend on.

Add to the mix that abstract beings exist necessarily and that they cannot depend on contingent concrete beings, and then arrive via a different route at our big conclusion: there is a necessary concrete being.

5.8 Parsimony

There are a few moving parts in Lowe's strategy, and critics can target any. Here we will focus on the view that

• the only abstract beings are properties and sets.

Lowe's attempt to reduce all candidate abstract beings to properties and sets is ambitious. Lots of philosophers try to reduce numbers to sets. For example, 0 has been taken to be the empty set, $\emptyset$, the 1 to be $\{\emptyset\}$, 2 to be $\{\{\emptyset\}\}$, and so on. Lowe prefers to reduce numbers to *properties* of sets (compare Huemer 2016: chapters 8 and 9). But how are we to begin modeling propositions or possibilities onto properties or sets?

Lowe actually requires something even more ambitious, that

• the only *possible* abstract beings are properties and sets.

But even if we can successfully reduce numbers, propositions, and possibilities to properties and sets, maybe there could be abstract beings that are not reducible – abstract beings we have no inkling of, abstract beings that do not actually exist but are possible. Then maybe these abstract beings could exist independently of any concrete beings. How can we rule this out?

Lowe tries reducing all abstract beings to sets and properties on the grounds of *parsimony*, as per

• Ockham's Razor: Do not postulate entities beyond necessity!

But the rule is usually applied to the actual, not the possible. We presume, partly on the basis of parsimony, that there are no unicorns. We do not presume, and not at all on the basis of parsimony, that there *could not* have been unicorns. David Efird and Tom Stoneham (2006: 277) even introduce a principle at odds with Ockham's Razor when it comes to possibilities:

• Hume's Razor: Do not multiply necessities beyond necessity!

By eliminating any possibility of alien abstract beings, we introduce the necessity of *no* alien abstract beings and violate Hume's Razor.

A general caution about parsimony principles: parsimony has been introduced as the final arbiter to decide in favor of, for example, modal realism as well as possibilism, idealism as well as materialism, and theism as well as atheism. The use of parsimony in supporting such opposite sides raises the suspicion that it is – half the time – not properly employed, and there are yet more general worries about applying parsimony in metaphysics (see Huemer 2009).

5.9 Mind

In the final step of his argument – what I have as premises 13 and 14 – Lowe argues that the abstract beings depend on intellect. But the mathematical objects outstrip our own intellectual capacities. So we invoke an infinite intellect to do the work:

> Putting these two thoughts together – (1) that necessary abstract beings, insofar as they are objects of reason, are "mind-dependent" beings, and (2) that they are dependent for their existence on a necessary concrete being – we are led to the conclusion that the being in question must be *a rational being with a mind* and, indeed, with a mind so powerful that it can comprehend all of mathematics and logic. (2012: 189–90)

While impressively infinite, the intellect need not be omnipotent, omnibenevolent, or even omniscient: the argument does not show that it comprehends anything beyond mathematics and logic. Another problem is that, so far as the argument goes, the infinite intellect need not be *one*. Perhaps the abstract beings depend on many intellects – even infinitely many, with one for each abstract being.

We might reply with Ockham's Razor: one infinite intellect is more parsimonious than infinitely many little intellects. And we might draw upon the relations between abstract beings too: for example, bigger numbers might include or contain smaller numbers. The idea is captured by

- Leibniz's definitions: 2 is 1 and 1, 3 is 2 and 1, 4 is 3 and 1, and so forth; and
- set theoretic constructions of the natural numbers: $3 = \{\{\{\emptyset\}\}\}, 2 = \{\{\emptyset\}\}, 1 = \{\emptyset\}$, and $0 = \emptyset$, as per Zermelo; $3 = \{\emptyset, \{\emptyset\}, \{\emptyset, \{\emptyset\}\}\}, 2 = \{\emptyset, \{\emptyset\}\}, 1 = \{\emptyset\}$, and $0 = \emptyset$, as per von Neumann.

This might mean that an intellect generating one abstract being (a bigger number) must thereby generate another abstract being (a smaller number). If so, then the intellect generating the one being (the bigger number) makes otiose another intellect generating the other being (the smaller number). There will always be unnecessary intellectual activity so long as we invoke an intellect that does not generate all the numbers, and Ockham's Razor cuts again (see Goldschmidt 2018).

A deeper problem is the assumption that abstract objects depend on intellect at all. Recall that Lowe tells us that the word *abstract* is a clue that abstract beings are "abstracted" or "drawn out" of a mind. But the original etiology of the word *abstract* is far from the definition of *abstract being* at work in Lowe's argument: a being that "does not exist in space or time" (2012: 180). Plantinga instead points to Adams, who argues for what we can call

- divine psychologism: abstract objects depend on God's intellect

in its advantages over the rivals:

- human psychologism: abstract objects depend on our intellects; they are ideas in human minds; and
- Platonism: abstract objects do not depend on any intellect; they are timeless and spaceless and float in Plato's heaven (see Adams 1994: chapter 7).

Against human psychologism, Frege (1960) levels famous objections – especially that on human psychologism,

- there would be finitely many numbers, since humans have only a finite number of ideas; and
- the numbers (and the mathematical truths depending on them) would be contingent,

whereas there must be infinitely many numbers and the truths of mathematics cannot be contingent. Even if we never existed and even if we thought otherwise, it would still be true that, for example, $2 + 2 = 4$. In contrast, divine psychologism does not face these objections. Since God is

- infinite, there could be infinitely many numbers; and
- a necessary being, the numbers could be necessary beings too.

Against Platonism, the big objections are that Platonism

- is not parsimonious: it saddles us with spooky objects; and, relatedly,
- undercuts our knowledge of mathematics: our intellects cannot make causal contact with such transcendent objects,

whereas on a causal theory of knowledge, causal contact is required for knowledge (see Benacerraf 1965). In contrast, divine psychologism does not face these problems. Since God is

- an intellect somewhat like ours, his ideas would be more familiar, less spooky than platonic objects; and
- omnipotent, he can forge the connection between his and our ideas

so that the numbers can make causal contact with our intellects, and our knowledge of mathematics is secured. Adams cites Leibniz: "just as God is the original source of all things, so also is all fundamental knowledge to be derived from God's knowledge, and in his light we see light" (1994: 187). Divine psychologism thus advertises advantages over human psychologism and Platonism on all fronts.

However, on closer inspection, divine psychologism faces some of the same problems. Just as human psychologism falters against the necessity of numbers and mathematics, so too does divine psychologism. For why must God necessarily have numerical and mathematical ideas? As *ideas*, could not God play around with them just as we can play around with our ideas? Assume he could. God might then imagine that the numbers do not exist or that they come together, for example, to make $2 + 2 = 5$. Mathematics again turns out to be contingent, which is absurd. So assume that God could not play around with the ideas. What then constrains the divine intellect? An answer: God's rational nature tracks something that is not up to him or anyone else. But now it looks like we are headed toward an independent mathematical reality – in the direction of Platonism and away from divine psychologism (see Goldschmidt 2018, connecting the problem to the "Euthyphro dilemma" and responses to that).

Additionally, a predilection for parsimony might count equally against divine psychologism just as against Platonism. The Platonist James Brown opens up that

> naturalist friends and colleagues enjoy teasing me (knowing I'm an atheist) along the lines that being a Platonist is really no different than believing in God. ... While I enjoy the kidding, I've actually never seen the slightest connection between religion and mathematical Platonism. But others have, including Lakoff and Núñez. ... The physicist turned theologian John Polkinhorne also sees a connection. ... Polkinghorne favourably cites a number of prominent mathematicians who are also Platonists (Gödel, Hardy, Connes) in support of the notion that mathematics is transcendent. God, of course, is transcendent, too, so, Polkinghorne seems to suggest, there is a kind of mutual support – Platonists should believe in God. (2012: 161; see Schneider 2017 for an ingenious puzzle for Brown's friends)

Brown dismisses the idea: "aside from transcendence, there is really no connection between belief in God and belief in a Platonic realm" (2012: 161). But, if the problem is about introducing transcendent objects, then Platonism and divine psychologism do face the same problem. To be sure, the divine psychologist (talk about pastoral care!) might reply that there is no problem of parsimony on divine psychologism since God is the simplest possible being and theism is the most parsimonious fundamental theory. The parsimony of theism is a tricky topic (see Swinburne 2004 for a sublime defense).

However that debate turns out, a big problem with the argument in favor of divine psychologism is that there are rival views Plantinga and Adams do not touch. Alternatives, such as fictionalism, do not postulate mathematical objects *at all* – neither human nor divine, neither psychological nor platonic (also see Gould 2014). But we already noted how Lowe's argument presupposes the existence of such objects. Let's not double count objections. We have enough.

5.10 Conclusion

Lowe advertises his argument as an ontological argument. It is armchair enough but quite different from the standard versions studied in the previous sections. Each of the premises has some plausibility, but there are a lot of premises to buy into, and we have discovered objections. There is another theistic argument that does not focus on the existence of numbers so much as on their applicability (see Steiner 1998). There is the idea that "[t]he miracle of the appropriateness of the language of mathematics for the formulation of the laws of physics is a wonderful gift which we neither understand nor deserve" (Wigner 1960, 14). While worthy of consideration, these are not ontological arguments, since they draw from empirical observations.

6 Others

Short books and lazy authors require a selective focus. I have focused on four ontological arguments. There are others. A few more are digested here, at decreasing length, highlighting just some of their salient features and problems. Figuring them out carefully is left for homework.

6.1 Anselm-Smith

A. D. Smith (2014) discovers an overlooked argument in Anselm's *Replies* to Gaunilo:

> Something than which a greater cannot be conceived cannot be conceived to exist except without a beginning. But whatever can be conceived to exist and does not exist can be conceived to exist with a beginning. Therefore, something than which a greater cannot be conceived cannot be conceived to exist and yet not exist. If, therefore, it can be conceived to exist, of necessity it exists. (trans in Smith 2014: 126)

The reasoning resembles an argument from Duns Scotus (1266–1308; see Scotus 1962: 50). Setting it out:

1. GOD cannot be conceived to exist with a beginning. (Premise)

2. Anything that can be conceived to exist but does not exist can be conceived to exist with a beginning. (Premise)
3. Therefore, either GOD cannot be conceived to exist or GOD exists. (From 1 and 2)
4. GOD can be conceived to exist. (Premise)
5. Therefore, GOD exists. (From 3 and 4)

Smith reconstructs a couple of arguments from Anselm for the "crucial premise" 2, including:

> Whatever can be conceived to exist and does not exist can be conceived not to exist.
> Whatever can be conceived not to exist is temporal in nature (i.e., necessarily, it would exist in time, or would be time).
> Whatever is temporal in nature and can be conceived as existing can be conceived as having a beginning.
> Therefore, whatever can be conceived to exist and does not exist can be conceived to exist with a beginning. (Smith 2014: 131)

Smith immediately worries about an objection from the

- essentiality of origins: beings could not have an origin different from the origin they do have

against the third *whatever*. Contrary to the premise, a temporal (exists in time) but eternal (has always existed) being could not have had a beginning, since then it would have had a different origin, contrary to the essentiality of origins.

Whether the essentiality of origins applies to eternal beings (they do not have origins, after all) and whether it is true in any case is doubtful (see Ahmed 2007: 45–54). But Smith avoids the objection by reworking the argument in terms of

- *kinds* – so that premise 2 will read something like: if there is no instance of a certain kind of being, something of that kind can be conceived with a beginning; and, following Anselm's lead,
- *ends* – so that premise 2 will read something like this: if there is no instance of a certain kind of being, something of that kind can be conceived with an end.

Yet Smith sees the premises as relying on a controversial neo-Platonism about eternity and temporality. So he settles on a reconstruction with a more modern feel:

1. For any essential kind of thing, if there is not, but possibly could be, something of that kind, then it is possible for something of that kind to be caused.
2. There possibly could be something divine (i.e., of the essential kind *divine*).
3. It is not possible for anything divine to be caused.

4. Therefore, something divine exists. (Smith 2014: 152, with premises numbered)

The crucial first premise is supported via a

- principle of sufficient reason: for every possible essential kind, something of the kind could have had a reason for its existence,

where "reason" does not mean *purpose*, but *cause* or *explanation* or something like that. Most versions of the principle tell us that the target beings *must* have a cause. But Smith's is more modest: even if you deny that a certain thing does have a cause, you might still admit that something of the same kind *could have* had a cause. The idea is that if there is not, but could have been, something of a certain kind, then something of that kind could have had a reason for its existence. Since the being does not exist necessarily, the reason could not be an "internal necessitating reason" (Smith 2014: 171) in its nature but would be an external cause, as per premise 1.

The argument will face objections over the

- principle of sufficient reason, even in its modest form;
- possibility of something divine (compare Sections 4.2–5); and
- threat of parodies and polytheism (compare Sections 2.8–9; 4.6).

On the last point, the argument might be reframed to apply to other uncausable beings, including other divine or nearly divine beings. Smith replies by sketching arguments against the possibility of other uncausable beings. For example, since the divine being (proven by the ontological argument) would be necessarily omnipotent, it *could* cause any other being, and since the divine being would exist necessarily, there could not be other uncausable beings.

The reply is not compelling – for omnipotence is supposed to cover only possible actions (see Section 4.4). If there could be other uncausable beings – beings that could not *possibly* be caused – then an omnipotent being need not be able to cause them. Smith merely gestures at an argument from Aquinas for the conclusion that there could not be other uncausable beings, but does not develop the argument (see Smith 2014: 173–74).

Versions of the principle of sufficient reason are at work in cosmological arguments from contingency. For a simple example, where the first premise is a version:

1. Every contingent fact has an explanation.
2. There is a contingent fact that includes all other contingent facts.
3. Therefore, there is an explanation of this fact.
4. This explanation must involve a necessary being.
5. This necessary being is God. (Pruss 2009: 25–6; numbering reformatted)

There are other versions (see, e.g., Pearce 2017). In addition to worries over the principle of sufficient reason (see Pruss 2006 for a defense), the big questions are usually over whether

- there is a relevantly inclusive contingent fact;
- the explanation must be in terms of a necessary being; and
- the necessary being must be God.

But, following Smith's lead, we might try to go with the more modest proposal that there *could have* been relevantly inclusive facts with explanations. Conjoin the provided premises and put in a big *possibly*:

1. Possibly 1, 2, 3, and 4.

From this, conclude that there possibly is a necessary and necessarily divine being:

2. Possibly 5.

By now the idea that the possibility of a necessary being gives us its actuality is familiar (see Section 4.1), and we can conclude that there is a necessary divine being. This strategy might be applied more generally to any argument for a necessary being; Maydole thus uses Aquinas's contingency argument toward a "quasi-ontological argument" (2009: 586; see Goldschmidt forthcoming).

This seems to be an advance. The more modest premise will still be controversial. Maybe whatever counts against the principle of sufficient reason or against a relevantly inclusive contingent fact counts against their possibility too. And a standard worry about cosmological arguments from contingency is that while they might show that there is a necessary being, even a powerful necessary being, they do not show that this being is God – omnipotent, omniscient, and omnibenevolent. If so, the updated argument similarly does not show that the necessary being is God (compare Section 5.1). The question of how far we can bridge the gap between necessary being and God – and from the armchair – is left for homework.

6.2 Leibniz-Gödel

Leibniz and Gödel present ontological arguments of their own, and both try to show the possibility of God via the *positivity* of divine attributes. Leibniz's argument is an expansion of Descartes's. Descartes cannot help himself to the premise that a perfect being has every perfection (see Section 3.2) until he shows that the perfect being is possible. Leibniz tries to fill the gap by showing that the perfections are compossible (i.e., can all be had together by the same being). He takes *perfections* to be properties that are

- simple: not reducible to or composed of other properties; and
- purely positive: having no negatives or limits.

Some properties *exclude* others. Having one means not having the other. For example, being square excludes being round. This is so because the properties are not simple or purely positive; their natures have composition and negatives. In contrast, simple and purely positive properties cannot interfere with each other in that way. As such, the perfections can all live happily together. A perfect being is possible (see Antognazza 2019).

Gödel's ontological argument is not an elaboration of Descartes's, but is more elaborate. It is based on various axioms and definitions (see Pruss 2018: 139–40, which I am following *very* closely):

- Axiom 1: A property A is positive if and only if its negation not-A is not positive;
- Axiom 2: If A is positive and A entails B, then B is positive; and
- Axiom 3: If A is positive, then necessarily A is positive,

where property A entails property B if necessarily anything having A has B too. For example, being red entails being colored. Then there is a definition of being

- God-like: something is God-like if and only if all its essential properties are positive and all positive properties are essential to it,

where a property is essential to a being if and only if it could not exist without that property. For example, mass is an essential property of a cat. With that introduced, there is

- Axiom 4: The property of being God-like is positive; and
- Axiom 5: The property of necessary existence is positive.

From these ingredients, Gödel first tries to prove that a necessarily existing God-like being is possible (compare Sections 4.2–5).

Crucial to the proof is an argument from Axioms 1 and 2 for the compossibility of positive properties. Assume (for *reductio*) that some positive properties A and B are not compossible. Then anything having A could not have B too; rather, necessarily anything having A has not-B. Thus, A entails not-B. Axiom 2 tells us that anything entailed by a positive property is positive. Thus, on the original assumption that A is positive, not-B is positive too. But Axiom 2 tells us that the negation of a positive property is not positive. Thus, on the original assumption, that B is positive, not-B is not positive. Contradiction! Contrary to the original assumption, positive properties must be compossible.

So positive properties can all live together, and, given Axioms 4 and 5, that includes God-likeness and necessary existence. So, a necessarily existing God-like being is possible. And there's the familiar move from the possibility of a necessary being to its actual existence.

Gödel's argument faces various objections (see, e.g., Sobel 2004) and requires various refinements (see Pruss 2018). Here's one problem – simple but not so positive – facing both Gödel and Leibniz. Even if their arguments work, they show only that a perfect being or a necessarily existing God-like being exists in some technical sense of *perfect* and *God-like*. Gödels's argument might show that *Göd* exists but not that God exists.

The traditional divine attributes are *positive* in some sense: they're well worth having. But the further step requires showing that they are *positive* in the relevant senses from Leibniz or Gödel. But neither Leibniz nor Gödel attempt as much. It's hard for us to take their lead because what they mean by *positive* is nebulous (but see Johnson 2004: 118–23; van Inwagen 2009). God is often taken to be, for example, unchanging (not changing), but would that be a positive property (see Priest 2018: 266)? Homework questions: What exactly is it for a property to be positive in the relevant senses, not to have limits or negatives? How might we test for this in the case of the divine attributes?

There are yet other arguments for compossibility. C'Zar Bernstein (2014) argues that if no being could have all perfections, then some perfections must be incompatible; having one perfection would rule out having some other perfection. Thus the perfection would make a being having it imperfect. But perfections cannot make beings imperfect. So, having one perfection could not rule out having another. Thus perfections are compossible.

But could not perfections make beings imperfect in the relevant way? After all, omnipotence would be a perfection even if it somehow ruled out omnibenevolence. The argument might *stipulate* that a perfection could not do that. Once again, further argument would be needed to show that divine attributes (or near enough; see Section 4.4–6) count as perfections in the relevant sense, and thus that the perfect being would be God.

6.3 Matthews-Baker

The argument from Gareth Matthews and Lynne Rudder Baker (2010) is supposed to be close to Anselm's in form, but distinguishes between

- unmediated causal powers: with these you can do things directly; and
- mediated causal powers: with these you cannot do things directly.

Unmediated causal powers make things *oomphy*. A fictional being like

> Pegasus has no unmediated causal powers, but he has mediated causal powers
> through the thoughts, depictions and literature in which he figures. In con-
> trast, those people who think about Pegasus, portray him in paintings and
> sculptures, and write stories about him themselves have unmediated causal
> powers. (Matthews & Baker 2010: 210)

If God is a mere idea or fiction, like Pegasus, then God has only mediated causal powers, like Pegasus's. But unmediated causal powers make things greater. So

> then a greater than God can be conceived, namely, something than which
> nothing greater can be conceived that actually has unmediated causal powers.
> According to you, something than which nothing greater can be conceived,
> by having only mediated causal powers, is something than which a greater
> can be conceived. By contradicting yourself in this way you have offered an
> indirect proof, that is, a *reductio ad absurdum*, that God, i.e. something than
> which nothing greater can be conceived, actually exists. (Matthews & Baker
> 2010: 211)

This argument is supposed to "skirt the difficult question of whether 'exists' is a genuine predicate" (2010: 210; see Section 3.7): mediated and unmediated causal powers certainly are properties. But the new argument does not avoid the other objections facing Anselm's argument – the island parody and so on (also see Oppy 2011, 2011a; Matthews & Baker 2011). Still, Matthews and Baker's paper is a neat dialogue in less than two pages – no big loss in reading it. Homework can be setting out their argument with numbered premises for practice of something or other.

6.4 Combinations

Nancy Cartwright worries about long arguments:

> In a *long argument* with many separate premises, the conclusion fails if any of
> its premises fail. No step in one of these arguments is likely to be entirely
> uncontroversial; each is at least a little dicey. The probability, then, that one or
> another, somewhere along the line, is false is significant. So why should we
> trust the conclusion, even if we cannot spot where the error lies? (2019: 92)

Interruption: Arguments with many crucial premises work in, for instance, mathematics, where all the premises are secure. But long arguments in philoso-phy are risky since the premises are shaky. Some ontological arguments are long: Lowe's argument has seven or eight assumed premises (see Section 5.1). And it's shaky for depending on so many (compare the long argument across Maydole 2009: 582–86). More generally:

I oppose
  Tall, skinny arguments that are sparse and tidy
In favor of arguments that are
  Short, stocky, and tangled.

'Stocky' is wide – the arguments cover a lot of the territory under the conclusion – and solid. I use 'tangled' to describe a rich network of inter-related arguments, each firmly attached to the ground, some with shared premises but where a great many also have a number of independent premises and, importantly, premises that come from a variety of different places outside the immediate domain in which the conclusion lives. (Cartwright 2019: 92)

Some ontological arguments are *short*. Descartes's simple reconstruction has only two premises (see Section 3.2). But it is hardly *stocky* or *tangled*. Yet there are stocky and tangled arguments for the existence of God. Swinburne (2004) draws from

- the existence of the universe for a cosmological argument;
- natural laws and their fine-tuning for a teleological argument;
- the connection of soul and body for an argument from consciousness; and
- apparent perceptions of God for an argument from religious experience.

Each piece is supposed to be just some evidence for the existence of God. Taken together, they are supposed to show the conclusion likely (see Poston 2018). The fingerprints, footprints, and DNA at the crime scene would each *independently* be just some evidence. But taken *together*, they can convict. Whether or not the case works, there is stockiness and tangledness.

Do ontological arguments add anything to the cumulative case? Some think so (see Arbour 2019). If the objections we have considered work, the idea is more like adding a zero. Do ontological arguments themselves accumulate to a case? The idea is more like adding zeros. Like other armchair proofs, ontological arguments are all-or-nothing: a failed ontological argument is no more evidence than is a failed mathematical "proof."

6.5 Conclusion

There remain other ontological arguments. My sense is that the same objections as those leveled in this book apply to those too. But perhaps not. Thank you for reading my little book.

References

Adams, Robert Merrihew (1994). *Leibniz: Determinist, Theist, Idealist*. New York: Oxford University Press.

Ahmed, Arif (2007). *Saul Kripke*. London: Bloomsbury.

Anselm (2001). *Proslogion: With the Replies of Gaunilo and Anselm*, Thomas Williams (trans.). Indianapolis: Hackett.

Antognazza, Maria Rosa (2018). "Leibniz." In Graham Oppy (ed.), *Ontological Arguments*. Cambridge: Cambridge University Press, 75–98.

Aquinas, Thomas. (2014). *Aquinas: Basic Works*, Jeffrey Hause & Robert Pasnau (eds.). Indianapolis: Hackett.

Arbour, Benjamin (2019). "Dogmatic Open-Mindedness and Open-Minded Dogmatics." In Gregory Trickett & John Gilhooly (eds.), *Open-Mindedness in Philosophy of Religion*. Newcastle upon Tyne: Cambridge Scholars, 76–99.

Arbour, Benjamin (n.d.). "Preserving Anselmian Monotheism: A Reply to Nagasawa." Unpublished manuscript.

Astell, Mary (2002). *A Serious Proposal to the Ladies*. Peterborough: Broadview.

Barnes, Jonathan (1972). *The Ontological Argument*. New York: St. Martin's Press.

Barth, Karl (1960). *Anselm: Fides Quaerens Intellectum*. Richmond: John Knox.

Benacerraf, Paul (1965). "What Numbers Could Not Be," *Philosophical Review* 74 (1): 47–73.

Bencivenga, Ermanno (1993). *Logic and Other Nonsense: The Case of Anselm and His God*. Princeton: Princeton University Press.

Bernstein, C'Zar (2014). "Giving the Ontological Argument Its Due," *Philosophia* 42 (3): 665–79.

Burns, Elizabeth (2018). "The Ontological Argument: Patching Plantinga's Ontological Argument by Making the Murdoch Move." In Trent Dougherty & Jerry Walls (eds.), *Two Dozen (or So) Arguments for God: The Plantinga Project*. New York: Oxford University Press, 123–36.

Brown, James Robert (2012). *Platonism, Naturalism, and Mathematical Knowledge*. New York: Routledge.

Byerly, Ryan (2010). The Ontomystical Argument Revisited. *International Journal for Philosophy of Religion* 67 (2): 95–105.

Campbell, Richard (2018). *Rethinking Anselm's Argument: A Vindication of his Proof of the Existence of God*. Leiden: Brill.

Cartwright, Nancy (2019). *Nature, the Artful Modeler: Lectures on Laws, Science, How Nature Arranges the World, and How We Can Arrange It Better*. Chicago: Open Court.

Chambers, Timothy (2000). "On Behalf of the Devil: A parody of Anselm Revisited," *Proceedings of the Aristotelian Society* 100 (1): 93–113.

Chandler, Hugh (1976). "Plantinga and the Contingently Possible," *Analysis*, 36 (2): 106–9.

Coggins, Geraldine (2010). *Could There Have Been Nothing? Against Metaphysical Nihilism*. New York: Palgrave Macmillan.

Collins, Robin (2018). "The Argument from Physical Constants: The Fine-Tuning for Discoverability." In Trent Dougherty & Jerry Walls (eds.), *Two Dozen (or So) Arguments for God: The Plantinga Project*. New York: Oxford University Press, 89–107.

Conee, Earl (2013). "Conceiving Absolute Greatness." In Tyron Goldschmidt (ed.), *The Puzzle of Existence: Why Is There Something Rather Than Nothing?* New York: Routledge, 110–27.

Conee, Earl (2005). "Why Not Nothing?" In Earl Conee & Ted Sider, *Riddles of Existence: A Guided Tour of Metaphysics*. Oxford: Oxford University Press.

Craig, William Lane (2018). "The Kalam Cosmological Argument." In Trent Dougherty & Jerry Walls (eds.), *Two Dozen (or So) Arguments for God: The Plantinga Project*. New York: Oxford University Press, 389–405.

Craig, William Lane (2016). *God over All: Divine Aseity and the Challenge of Platonism*. Oxford: Oxford University Press.

Dawkins, Richard (2006). *The God Delusion*. New York: Houghton Mifflin.

Dennett, Daniel (2006). *Breaking the Spell: Religion as a Natural Phenomenon*. New York: Penguin.

Descartes, René (1986). *Meditations on First Philosophy: With Selections from the Objections and Replies*. John Cottingham (trans.). Cambridge: Cambridge University Press.

Descartes, René (1984). *The Philosophical Writings of Descartes: Volume II*. John Cottingham, Robert Stoothoff, & Dugald Murdoch (trans.). Cambridge: Cambridge University Press.

Dicker, Georges (2013). *Descartes: An Analytical and Historical Introduction* (2nd ed.). Oxford: Oxford University Press.

Efird, David, & Stoneham, Tom (2006). "Combinatorialism and the Possibility of Nothing," *Australasian Journal of Philosophy* 84 (2): 269–80.

Field, Hartry (1980). *Science without Numbers*. Princeton: Princeton University Press.

Francks, Richard (2008). *Descartes's Meditations: A Reader's Guide*. New York: Continuum.

Frege, Gottlob (1960). *The Foundations of Arithmetic.* J. L. Austin (trans.). New York: Harper.

Gale, Richard (1991). *On the Nature and Existence of God.* Cambridge: Cambridge University Press.

Gellman, Jerome (1997). *Experience of God and the Rationality of Theistic Belief.* Ithaca: Cornell University Press.

Goldschmidt, Tyron (forthcoming). "Ontological Soufflé," *Ratio.*

Goldschmidt, Tyron (2019). "A Proof of Exodus: Yehuda HaLevi and Jonathan Edwards Walk Into a Bar." In Samuel Lebens, Dani Rabinowitz, & Aaron Segal (eds.), *Jewish Philosophy in an Analytic Age.* Oxford: Oxford University Press, 222–42.

Goldschmidt, Tyron (2018). "The Argument From Numbers'. In Trent Dougherty & Jerry Walls (eds.), *Two Dozen (or So) Arguments for God: The Plantinga Project.* New York:Oxford University Press, 59–75.

Gould, Paul (2014). *Beyond the Control of God? Six Views on the Problem of God and Abstract Objects.* New York: Bloomsbury.

Hartshorne, Charles (1962). *The Logic of Perfection.* La Salle: Open Court.

Hoffman, Joshua, & Rosenkrantz, Gary (2002). *The Divine Attributes.* New York: Wiley-Blackwell.

Huemer, Michael (2016). *Approaching Infinity.* New York: Palgrave Macmillan.

Huemer, Michael (2009). "When Is Parsimony a Virtue?," *Philosophical Quarterly* 59 (235): 216–36.

Huemer, Michael (2005). *Ethical Intuitionism.* New York: Palgrave Macmillan.

Hume, David (1998). *Dialogues Concerning Natural Religion.* Richard Popkin (ed.). Indianapolis: Hackett.

Johnson, David (2004). *Truth without Paradox.* Landham: Roman and Littlefield.

Kant, Immanuel (1998). *Critique of Pure Reason.* Paul Guyer & Allen Wood (trans.).Cambridge: Cambridge University Press.

Kraay, Klaas (2010). "Theism, Possible Worlds, and the Multiverse," *Philosophical Studies* 147 (3): 355–68.

Kwan, Kai-man (2009). "The Argument from Religious Experience." In William Lane Craig & J. P. Moreland (eds.), *The Blackwell Companion to Natural Theology.* Oxford: Blackwell, 498–552.

Leftow, Brian (2018). "Aquinas" In Graham Oppy (ed.), *Ontological Arguments.* Cambridge: Cambridge University Press, 44–52.

Leftow, Brian (1988). "Anselmian Polytheism," *International Journal for Philosophy of Religion* 23 (2): 77–104

Leng, Mary (ed.) (2010). *Mathematics and Reality.* Oxford: Oxford University Press.

Lewis, David (1970). "Anselm and Actuality," *Noûs* 4 (2): 175–88.

Logan, Ian (2008). *Reading Anselm's Proslogion: The History of Anselm's Argument and Its Significance Today.* London: Ashgate.

Lowe, E. J. (2013). "The Ontological Argument." In Chad Meister & Paul Copan (eds.), *The Routledge Companion to Philosophy of Religion.* New York: Routledge, 391–400.

Lowe, E. J. (2012). "A New Modal Version of the Ontological Argument." In Mirosaw Szatkowski (ed.), *Ontological Proofs Today.* Frankfurt: Ontos Verlag, 179–91.

Lowe, E. J. (1998). *The Possibility of Metaphysics: Substance, Identity, and Time.* Oxford: Oxford University Press.

Lycan, William (2019). *On Evidence in Philosophy.* Oxford: Oxford University Press.

Malcolm, Norman (1960). "Anselm's Ontological Arguments," *Philosophical Review* 69 (1): 41–62.

Marek, Johann (2019). "Alexius Meinong," *Stanford Encyclopedia of Philosophy.* https://plato.stanford.edu/entries/meinong/

Matthews, Gareth, & Baker, Lynne Rudder (2010). "The Ontological Argument Simplified," *Analysis* 70 (2): 210–12.

Matthews, Gareth, & Baker, Lynne Rudder (2011). "Reply to Oppy's Fool," *Analysis* 71(2): 303.

Mavrodes, George (1963). "Some Puzzles Concerning Omnipotence," *Philosophical Review* 72 (2): 221–23.

Maydole, Robert (2009). "The Ontological Argument." In William Lane Craig & J. P. Moreland (eds.), *The Blackwell Companion to Natural Theology.* Oxford: Blackwell, 553–92.

McGinnis, Jon (2011). "The Ultimate Why Question: Avicenna on Why God Is Absolutely Necessary." In John Wippel (ed.), *The Ultimate Why Question: Why Is There Anything at All Rather Than Nothing Whatsoever?* Washington: Catholic University of America Press, 65–83.

Millican, Peter (2004). "The One Fatal Flaw in Anselm's Argument," *Mind* 113 (451): 437–76.

Millican, Peter (2007). "Ontological Arguments and the Superiority of Existence: Reply to Nagasawa," *Mind* 116 (464): 1041–105.

Miravalle, John-Mark (2018). *God, Existence, and Fictional Objects: The Case for Meinongian Theism.* New York: Bloomsbury Academic.

Morris, Thomas (1987). *Anselmian Explorations: Essays in Philosophical Theology.* Notre Dame: University of Notre Dame Press.

Morriston, Wes (2001). "Omnipotence and Necessary Moral Perfection: Are They Compatible?," *Religious Studies* 37 (2): 143–60.

Nagasawa, Yujin (2017). *Maximal God: A New Defence of Perfect Being Theism*. Oxford: Oxford University Press.

Nagasawa, Yujin (2007). "Millican on the Ontological Argument," *Mind* 116 (464): 1027–39.

Naylor van Inwagen, Margery (1969). *Descartes' Three Versions of the Ontological Argument*. Unpublished doctoral dissertation, University of Rochester, Rochester, NY.

Nolan, Lawrence (2018). "Descartes." In Graham Oppy (ed.), *Ontological Arguments*. Cambridge: Cambridge University Press, 53–74.

O'Connor, Timothy (2008). *Theism and Ultimate Explanation: The Necessary Shape of Contingency*. Oxford: Wiley-Blackwell.

Oppy, Graham (ed.) (2018). *Ontological Arguments*. Cambridge: Cambridge University Press.

Oppy, Graham (2018). "Introduction: Ontological Arguments in Focus." In Graham Oppy (ed.), *Ontological Arguments*. Cambridge: Cambridge University Press, 1–18.

Oppy, Graham (2011). "Objection to a Simplified Ontological Argument," *Analysis* 71(1): 105–6.

Oppy, Graham (2011a). "On Behalf of the Fool," *Analysis*, 71 (2): 304–6.

Oppy, Graham (2009). "Pruss's Ontological Arguments," *Religious Studies* 45 (3): 355–63.

Oppy, Graham (1995). *Ontological Arguments and Belief in God*. Cambridge: Cambridge University Press.

Parsons, Terence (1980). *Nonexistent Objects*. New Haven: Yale University Press.

Pearce, Kenneth (2017). "Foundational Grounding and the Argument from Contingency," *Oxford Studies in Philosophy of Religion* 8.

Plantinga, Alvin (2007). "Two Dozen (or So) Theistic Arguments." In Deane-Peter Baker (ed.), *Alvin Plantinga*. Cambridge: Cambridge University Press, 203–28.

Plantinga, Alvin (1974). *God, Freedom, and Evil*. Grand Rapids: Eerdmans.

Plantinga, Alvin (1974a). *The Nature of Necessity*. Oxford: Clarendon Press.

Poston, Ted (2018). "The Argument from (A) to (Y): The Argument from So Many Arguments." In Trent Dougherty & Jerry Walls (eds.), *Two Dozen (or So) Arguments for God: The Plantinga Project*. New York: Oxford University Press, 372–86.

Priest, Graham (2018). "Characterization, Existence and Necessity." In Graham Oppy (ed.), *Ontological Arguments*. Cambridge: Cambridge University Press, 250–69.

Pruss, Alexander (2018). "Gödel." In Graham Oppy (ed.), *Ontological Arguments*. Cambridge: Cambridge University Press, 139–54.

Pruss, Alexander (2009). "The Leibnizian Cosmological Argument." In William Lane Craig & J. P. Moreland (eds.), *The Blackwell Companion to Natural Theology*. Oxford: Blackwell, 24–100.

Pruss, Alexander (2006). *The Principle of Sufficient Reason: A Reassessment*. Cambridge: Cambridge University Press.

Pruss, Alexander (2001). "Śamkara's Principle and Two Ontomystical Arguments," *International Journal for Philosophy of Religion* 49 (2): 111–20.

Pruss, Alexander, & Rasmussen, Joshua (2018). *Necessary Existence*. Oxford: Oxford University Press.

Rasmussen, Joshua (2018). "Plantinga." In Graham Oppy (ed.), *Ontological Arguments*. Cambridge: Cambridge University Press, 176–94.

Reicher, Maria (2019). "Nonexistent Objects," *Stanford Encyclopedia of Philosophy*. https://plato.stanford.edu/entries/nonexistent-objects/

Rizvi, Sajjad (2019). "Mulla Sadra," *Stanford Encyclopedia of Philosophy*. https://plato.stanford.edu/entries/mulla-sadra/

Rowe, William (2009). "Alvin Plantinga on the Ontological Argument," *International Journal for Philosophy of Religion* 65 (2), 87–92.

Rowe, William (1987). "Modal Versions of the Ontological Argument." In Louis Pojman (ed.), *Philosophy of Religion: An Anthology*. Wadsworth: Balmont, 69–73.

Rowe, William (1976). "The Ontological Argument and Question-Begging," *International Journal for Philosophy of Religion* 7 (4): 425–32.

Russell, Bertrand (2004). *History of Western Philosophy*. London: Routledge.

Russell, Bertrand (1905). "On Denoting," *Mind* 14 (56): 479–93.

Schneider, Susan (2017). "Idealism, or Something Near Enough." In Tyron Goldschmidt & Kenneth Pearce (eds.), *Idealism: New Essays in Metaphysics*. Oxford: Oxford University Press, 275–89.

Scotus, Duns (1962). *Philosophical Writings*. Allan Wolter (trans.). Indianapolis: Bobbs-Merrill.

Sinnott-Armstrong, Walter (1999). "Begging the Question," *Australasian Journal of Philosophy* 77 (2): 174–91.

Smith, A. D. (2014). *Anselm's Other Argument*. Harvard: Harvard University Press.

Sobel, Jordan Howard (2004). *Logic and Theism: Arguments for and against Belief in God*. Cambridge: Cambridge University Press.

Sorensen, Roy (1991). "'P, therefore, P' without Circularity," *Journal of Philosophy* 88 (5): 245–66.

Speaks, Jeff (2018). *The Greatest Possible Being*. Oxford: Oxford University Press.

Spinoza, Baruch (1992). *Ethics*. Indianapolis: Hackett.

Stang, Nicholas (2016). *Kant's Modal Metaphysics*. Oxford: Oxford University Press.

Stang, Nicholas (2015). "Kant's Argument That Existence Is Not a Determination," *Philosophy and Phenomenological Research* 91 (1): 583–626.

Steiner, Mark (1998). *The Applicability of Mathematics as a Philosophical Problem*. Cambridge: Harvard University Press.

Street, Sharon (2006). "A Darwinian Dilemma for Realist Theories of Value," *Philosophical Studies* 127 (1):109–66.

Streumer, Bart (2017). *Unbelievable Errors*. Oxford: Oxford University Press.

Swinburne, Richard (2016). *The Coherence of Theism* (2nd ed.). Oxford: Oxford University Press.

Swinburne, Richard (2012). "What Kind of Necessary Being Could God Be?" In Mirosaw Szatkowski (ed.), *Ontological Proofs Today*. Frankfurt: Ontos Verlag, 345–63.

Swinburne, Richard (2004). *The Existence of God* (2nd ed.). Oxford: Oxford University Press.

Szatkowski, Miroslaw (ed.) (2012). *Ontological Proofs Today*. Frankfurt: Ontos Verlag.

Thomasson, Amie (1998). *Fiction and Metaphysics*. Cambridge: Cambridge University Press.

Van Inwagen, Peter (2018). "Begging the Question." In Graham Oppy (ed.), *Ontological Arguments*. Cambridge: Cambridge University Press, 238–49.

Van Inwagen, Peter (2012). "Three Versions of the Ontological Argument." In Mirosaw Szatkowski (ed.), *Ontological Proofs Today*. Frankfurt: Ontos Verlag, 143–62.

Van Inwagen, Peter (2009). "Some Remarks on Modal Ontological Arguments," *Philo* 12 (2): 217–27.

Van Inwagen, Peter (2006). *The Problem of Evil*. Oxford: Oxford University Press.

Van Inwagen, Peter (2001). "Existence, Ontological Commitment, and Fictional Entities." In Michael Loux & Dean Zimmerman (eds.), *The Oxford Handbook of Metaphysics*. Oxford: Oxford University Press, 131–57.

Visser, Sandra, & Williams, Thomas (2008). *Anselm*. Oxford: Oxford University Press.

Weiss, Roslyn (2017). "Waiting for Godo . . . and Godan: Completing Rowe's Critique of the Ontological Argument," *European Journal for Philosophy of Religion* 9 (1): 65–86.

Wigner, Eugene (1960). "The Unreasonable Effectiveness of Mathematics in the Natural Sciences," *Communications in Pure and Applied Mathematics* 13: 1–14.

Williams, Thomas (2016). "Anselm's Proslogion," *Topoi* 35 (2): 613–6.

Wilson, Catherine (2003). *Descartes's Meditations: An Introduction*. Cambridge: Cambridge University Press.

Acknowledgments

Thanks to Stevan Apter, Ben Arbour, C'Zar Berntstein, Kevin Gausselin, Hud Hudson, Liz Jackson, Klaas Kraay, Samuel Lebens, Yujin Nagasawa, Graham Oppy, Sajjad Rizvi, Josef Stern, and Craig Warmke for comments or discussion. Thanks especially to Joshua Rasmussen, Aaron Segal, and Roslyn Weiss for detailed comments on the draft. For Hannah.

Cambridge Elements ⁼

Philosophy of Religion

Yujin Nagasawa

University of Birmingham

Yujin Nagasawa is Professor of Philosophy and Co-Director of the John Hick Centre for Philosophy of Religion at the University of Birmingham. He is currently President of the British Society for the Philosophy of Religion. He is a member of the Editorial Board of *Religious Studies*, the *International Journal for Philosophy of Religion* and *Philosophy Compass*.

About the Series

This Cambridge Elements series provides concise and structured introductions to all the central topics in the philosophy of religion. It offers balanced, comprehensive coverage of multiple perspectives in the philosophy of religion. Contributors to the series are cutting-edge researchers who approach central issues in the philosophy of religion. Each provides a reliable resource for academic readers and develops new ideas and arguments from a unique viewpoint.

Cambridge Elements ≡

Philosophy of Religion

Elements in the Series

A full series listing is available at: www.cambridge.org/EPREL

Printed in the United States
By Bookmasters